IT IS JUST YOU

EVERYTHING'S NOT SHIT

IT IS JUST YOU

EVERYTHING'S NOT SHIT

Steve Stack

FRIDAY BOOKS

First published in Great Britain in 2007 by Friday Books

An imprint of The Friday Project Limited

83 Victoria Street, London SW1H 0HW

www.thefridayproject.co.uk

www.fridaybooks.co.uk

ISBN – 978-1-905548-67-5

British Library Cataloguing in Publication Data

A catalogue record for this book is available from the British Library

Cover and Internal Design by Snowbooks Design

www.snowbooksdesign.com

Printed by MPG Books Ltd.

The Publisher's policy is to use paper manufactured from sustainable sources

for

you know who

with love

x

Introduction

In recent years there have been a number of popular books moaning about life and how crap it is. Whether it be grumpy old men, miserable old women, or people asking, 'Is it just me or is everything shit?'. I am OK with that, I accept that the world can be a crappy place sometimes, but do we have to be so bloody pessimistic?

I am a fully paid-up subscriber to the notion that life is actually pretty damn great. There are loads of wonderful people, places and experiences surrounding us every moment of our lives and if we ignore that fact, then it is no wonder that we end up grumpy and miserable.

This book is designed to celebrate what is good in life and to act as a reminder that there are truly great things to experience all around us. I have tried to select an array of subjects that should inspire, delight, fill us with wonder or just make us smile. From the humble, but highly amusing aardvark to the altruistic global vision of Nobel Peace Prize winner Muhamad Yunus; from breakfast in bed to Patrick Moore playing the xylophone; I hope the following entries present the case for the nice things in life.

But whatever you do, don't take it too seriously.

Steve Stack
(from my hammock in the garden)
2007

Aardvark

Whether you are an ardent Creationist or zealous advocate of Darwinism you have to admit that the aardvark is one amazing creature. Weighing in at up to 150lb and with a nose like a Clanger, the aardvark is almost entirely hairless and can seal its nostrils at will.

The unusual name comes from the Afrikaans for 'earth pig' and makes it ideally placed for coming at the beginning of encyclopedias, much to the envy of yaks and zebras. Native to Africa, the aardvark is no relation to the anteater, in fact it doesn't eat ants at all – it eats termites, often by sucking them straight out of the ground. An accomplished digger, it can burrow through even quite hard earth, but generally it can't be bothered, moving on to softer stuff elsewhere. Not that it is a lazy animal, far from it; when an aardvark first wakes up it leaps around for 30 feet or so before going about its business. And when attacked, it will use its strong tail to somersault out of harm's way.

Put Richard Dawkins and Pope Gregory XVI in a room, show them a picture of an aardvark and for a brief moment they will be united in appreciation at the sheer wonder of such an animal. And then they'd spend the rest of the night arguing about just who made it.

FASCINATING FACT

The collective noun for aardvarks is *aarmory*, although some experts disagree on this. Not that they have ever offered an alternative so they should probably keep quiet.

Advent calendars

Why restrict the joy of Christmas to one solitary day when you could extend it to cover the twenty-four preceding ones as well? All you need to do is hang up a sheet of cardboard with little windows cut into it. Easy.

For some reason, pulling open the little hinged flaps to reveal the picture and – if you are middle-class and not related to a dentist – chocolate hidden behind is a minor miracle every December morning. Just watch parents volunteering to assist children who are having trouble getting theirs open.

The first advent calendar was made in either Austria or Germany in the early part of the twentieth century. The Austrians and Germans can't seem to decide who got there first, while the rest of the world thinks of them as pretty much the same country, anyway, so isn't that fussed. Before printed calendars, families would light an advent candle (some still do) or mark the twenty-four days off with chalk marks on the fireplace (slightly less popular now).

Allotments

You might find it odd to see an entry for allotments in a book about all things nice and wonderful but there is a very good reason for their inclusion. Put simply, if it weren't for allotments you probably wouldn't be here today. During the Second World War, when the UK was blockaded by U-boats, the women, children and old men of the nation picked up their spades as part of the 'Dig for Victory' campaign. The 1.4 million allotment plots across the land yielded 1.3 million tonnes of produce a year – that's nearly 1 tonne per plot! The fruit and veg grown on small pieces of council land fed your parents, grandparents or great-grandparents and led to you sitting (or standing) there right now holding this book.

The idea of allotments – small areas of council or parish land given over to local residents for them to grow fruit, vegetables and flowers – dates back over two hundred years but they really came into their own during Victorian times. As more and more families moved to the cities, less and less agricultural land was being tended and the new urban dwellers were encouraged to 'grow their own'. It was also seen as a way to keep the lower classes occupied and off the demon drink.

Since the end of the Second World War, the number of allotments in the UK has decreased to around 250,000 and many feared that the decline was terminal. However, allotment land is protected by an Act of Parliament and councils are obliged to keep the space available at low rents to residents. Thankfully, the last few years have seen a resurgence in allotment use from young gardeners and their families moving towards a more environmentally conscious philosophy as the appetite for organic produce increases. So they are likely to be around for a long time to come.

Allotment shows

And if it were not for allotments then we would never have had allotment shows: old men showing off award-winning onions and dusting down their leeks alongside young whippersnappers with enormous pumpkins. Even the most cynical of observers cannot fail to be enthralled by the politics and etiquette of prize vegetables.

Amuse bouche

In some of the more posh restaurants your meal will begin with an unannounced course, known as an *amuse bouche* (literally, 'mouth amuser' or 'to amuse the mouth'). This is usually a small appetiser designed to titillate your taste buds.

So, let's get this straight. We are talking about a surprise extra course, at no additional charge, specifically designed to make you smile before embarking upon the main meal. What's not to like?

Archers theme tune

Tum ti-tum ti-tum ti-tum
Tum ti-tum ti ta tum...

Even if you don't listen to *The Archers*, or even Radio 4, you can probably hum the opening bars of the theme tune. One of the most instantly recognisable pieces of music in contemporary culture, it has heralded the start of this agricultural soap opera since it began in 1950. A particularly joyful ditty, Billy Connolly once suggested it should be adopted as the UK's national anthem.

The original composition is called *Barwick Green*, written by Arthur Wood. It is taken from his suite *My Native Heath* where it features as a maypole dance. And perhaps that explains the enduring appeal: to have a jaunty country tune explode onto the airwaves immediately after a depressing news report can put the supposed ills of this world into perspective.

Arts cinemas

They might show far more subtitled movies than are good for them but any cinema that serves a cup of tea and slice of cake that you can take into the auditorium with you is worthy of celebration. Watching angst-ridden French actors argue with each other in between bouts of athletic and graphic sex is made all the more palatable with a forkful of cream slice. Try it some time.

Sir David Attenborough

Sir David Attenborough is worthy of two entries in this book – one for his remarkable body of work and another for the wonderfully soothing effect of his voice – but I shall combine both here.

He has been broadcasting on television since 1954 and his career since then has spanned twenty separate series, with a twenty-first currently in production, and countless individual documentaries. His perceptive, empathetic and enthralling commentary to each of these programmes has been one of the major factors in their enduring quality and generations of children and adults have grown up listening to his voice. He has informed, educated and delighted an entire nation.

FASCINATING FACT

Attenborough's groundbreaking 1979 series, *Life on Earth* was watched by over 500 million people worldwide when originally broadcast.

Bacon sandwiches

Proof of the irresistible nature of the bacon sandwich is that it stands as the number one reason for former vegetarians falling off the wagon. Even hardened veggies (you know, the ones who don't even eat fish) can be seen to swoon at the smell of frying bacon and the sight of a bread knife cutting through a crusty loaf in preparation. I once lived with a woman who had been vegetarian all her life (I blame the parents) but still insisted on making my bacon sandwiches for me so that she could be close to their sheer culinary perfection.

Bacon sandwiches come in all shapes and sizes, with many accompanying ingredients, but – and here is the ultimate accolade – they are all great. A long, crunchy baguette filled with exotic salad and slaverings of mayonnaise can be delightful, but then no connoisseur of the bacon butty would turn down two slices of white with a bit of butter and brown sauce either. It doesn't matter how you serve it up, a bacon sandwich is bloody marvellous.

Everyone who makes a bacon sandwich will claim to be the finest proponent of the art in the whole of Christendom. I am no exception and here is my classic recipe:

- 3 rashers of smoked back bacon (it is worth stumping up for some really good quality stuff from a proper butcher but, let's face it, anything will do)
- 2 slices of hand-cut crusty white bread
- some rocket leaves
- a handful of cherry tomatoes, cut in half
- Parmesan cheese
- mayonnaise
- Dijon mustard
- some butter (obviously)

Fry the bacon in a little olive oil. When the bacon is almost cooked, but not quite at the crispy stage, chuck in some cherry tomatoes. While these are cooking you can prepare the bread.Cut two thick slices and slap on the butter. Coat one slice with a generous amount of mayonnaise, and the other with an equally friendly spreading of mustard. Using the mayo slice as your base, pile on the rocket leaves (as much as you want, really). Once the bacon is crispy enough for you, then arrange the slices on the bread; I prefer two diagonal and once across the middle. Plonk the cooked tomatoes on top and then, using a potato peeler, shave some Parmesan over the lot where it will start to melt. Stick the mustard slice on top and press down firmly. Cut lengthways (never diagonally – too flimsy) and enjoy with a cup of tea, a broad grin and juices dribbling down your chin.

Bank Holidays

Any day when you don't have to go into work is good. But here's the remarkable thing about Bank Holidays – there is no legal right to time off, but we get to stay home anyway.

Originally, in the eighteenth and nineteenth centuries, Bank Holidays were just that: days when the banks were closed. There were thirty to forty of them spread across the year coinciding with religious festivals and feast days but only bank employees really benefited from them.

It wasn't until 1871, when Sir John Lubbock introduced the Bank Holidays Act, that the rest of us got a lie-in as well. Lubbock was a wonderful old duffer who felt that bank employees should be allowed to watch lots of cricket, so his list of holidays included the dates when village matches tended to be played.

There has been plenty of fiddling with the numbers, frequency and timing of Bank Holidays since the original Act of Parliament and many people are lobbying for a few more days to be chucked into the mix as well. Most popular are the arguments for St George's, St Andrew's and St David's days for England, Scotland and Wales respectively, in line with the national day of drinking and falling over in Ireland for St Patrick's Day.

FASCINATING FACT

Christmas Day and Good Friday are not technically Bank Holidays, although they are observed as common law holidays.

Albert Coombs Barnes

Every now and again, history throws up an individual so eccentric and remarkable that they deserve to become part of modern folklore. Albert Coombs Barnes is one such person, but sadly his renown is nowhere near as great as it should be.

Barnes was born in 1872 in Philadelphia in America, the son of a butcher. He paid his own way through university where he excelled in chemistry. As a young man he developed a treatment for gonorrhoea (rumour had it to cure his own) that proved so successful that he was able to retire, a millionaire, at the age of 35.

He subsequently founded the Barnes Foundation, which acted as an art collection and cultural centre. He also funded projects for the underprivileged of his home city. And he certainly knew his art from his elbow, since the Foundation included works by Picasso, Modigliani, Matisse and a number of Renoirs, many of which he had bought for bargain prices.

Access to this formidable art collection could only be achieved by writing to Barnes to request permission. Applicants who had, for whatever reason, incurred the ire of the great man would often receive rejection letters from Barnes' dog, Fidele. Here is one such letter:

Madame,
I have received your letter of the -th, asking for leave to visit my master's Foundation.
Unhappily, being young and poor, my master was treated in a hospital founded by your family. As a result of intimate relations with one of the

nurses he contracted a venereal disease. He has never forgotten this, and is therefore obliged to refuse your request.

He was also a strong supporter of the black rights movement in America and would frequently receive visitors of all colours at his home in Philadelphia. When this brought protests from his neighbours (this was 1930s America), he pointed out that he owned the land they lived on and threatened to build a hospital for the black community right in the middle of the richest district in town. This soon shut them up.

My favourite Barnes story was when a rich socialite couple came to visit the Foundation. They were met by a janitor who was busy washing the floors. They then proceeded to loudly criticise the Renoirs and Cezannes on display, at which point the janitor manhandled them off the premises. He, of course, turned out to be Barnes himself.

Baths
With any combination of the following:

a) a glass of wine
b) bubbles
c) a good book
d) someone else

Bedtime stories
When I was a child, I would look forward to bedtime and hearing the magical stories my parents would read from books or make up off the top of their heads. It was one of the highlights of my day.

Now, as a parent, I find myself looking forward to my children's bedtime so that I can read them stories or make some up myself. It is *absolutely* the highlight of my day.

Bekonscot Model Village

At the very end of the walk round Bekonscot Model Village there is a sign. It isn't particularly big but its size is in inverse proportion to the joy it brings to those who read it. It says, quite simply:

Please feel free to walk round again.

Roland Callingham was a successful London accountant in the 1920s and with the money he made from his business he bought several acres of meadows adjoining his home in Beaconsfield in Buckinghamshire. Together with his head gardener, Tom Berry, he built a number of model houses as a feature for his alpine garden. The scale he used for these houses (1 inch to 1 foot) is now the accepted 1:12 scale for all dolls houses worldwide.

In the early days, the model village was only intended to entertain his friends and clients but, as it grew in size, he was encouraged to open it to the public. He did so in 1929 and Bekonscot Model Village was born – the first such attraction in the world. During his lifetime Callingham added an extensive railway system, a lake and a number of surrounding villages, including Greenhaily with its own zoo and the fishing village of Southpool.

Nearly eighty years later, Bekonscot is still going strong with all proceeds given to charity. A decision was taken in 1993 to maintain the village in its 1930s likeness, thus preserving a portrait of a way of life that has long since vanished in the real world.

Being a kid for five minutes

Sometimes the opportunity presents itself to shrug off your adult years and muck in with the kids. Setting up a Scalextric set, finger painting, rearranging the furniture in a dolls' house, rolling out plasticine, making mud pies. The list will differ depending on your age and what you got up to when you were a child, but the unadulterated joy of these stolen moments is the same for everyone.

Berry picking

Few foods taste nicer than a blackberry picked from the bramble and popped straight into the mouth, or a strawberry plucked by hand. Modern retailing means that you can buy most types of berry, frozen or fresh(ish) all year round, but not even the owners of Tesco would claim that a raspberry flown over from South Africa tastes as good as one you have picked yourself.

Pick-Your-Own farms are commonplace and scattered across the UK. At the height of summer they are full of seasoned pickers and children toddling around with juice-stained faces. Obviously the aforementioned raspberries and strawberries are popular, as are gooseberries for cooking, but there are many more berries out there to try:

Bilberry. A pain in the backside to harvest but they are very tasty and well worth the bother if you have the patience. They are the key ingredient of Mucky Mouth Pies, a popular Yorkshire dish.

Cloudberry. Largely native (in the form of jam) to IKEA stores nowadays, you can still find this small shrub alongside moors in the north of England and across Scotland, although they are quite scarce. If you are lucky enough to come across some of these deep orange berries, they taste great warmed over ice cream or used in puddings or jam.

Cowberry. A close relative of the cranberry, these really need to be cooked before eating.

Crowberry. You are unlikely to find many of these around (they are far more common in Scandinavia), but they make a nice jelly.

Dewberry. A little like a small blackberry, but with less of a cluster of fruit; these are very difficult to pick without bursting, so it is best to snip the stems and then eat the fruit dipped in sugar.

Juneberry. Quite rare and usually confined to the south of England, these are sweet purple berries and can be eaten straight from the bush.

Rowanberry. Found on the rowan tree, or mountain ash, these resemble elderberries but are larger and bright orange. They are usually cooked and preserved as jam or served as a sauce with meat and game.

Whitebeam. You can often find these on suburban roadsides and they are also a popular garden shrub. The small bunches of red berries are not overly nice, but at least you can say you tried them.

Birthday cards with cash in them

When you are a child, cards are the most boring part of birthdays. What you want are presents, and lots of them. So when you open up that pastel-coloured envelope to reveal a card with a puppy on it, you have to pretend to be grateful. But then a nice crisp tenner falls out and suddenly the moment is saved. We've all been there, don't pretend you haven't.

Black and white movies

Sunday afternoon, no one in the house, black and white movie* on the telly, bar of chocolate on the arm of the sofa. Perfection.

Bookshop browsing

Some of the greatest pleasures in life are the most simple. Standing in a bookshop, surrounded by thousands of volumes, is one such joy.

Ideally, you would be in no rush. It is good to linger when browsing books. You can then identify a suitable section and decide upon your strategy. There are many to choose from:

The Librarian. Strict alphabetical order; you start at A and allow your eye to run across each spine, perhaps aided by a pointing finger. A small *"Tut!"* may venture from your lips when you find something not in the correct order. Selected books will be removed from the shelf, examined and then placed back carefully

---

*It makes absolutely no difference what the film is, as long as it is in black and white.

from whence they came. After twenty minutes you have only reached as far as C, so make a mental note of where you got to for your next visit.

The ADHD. Even though you have all the time in the world, you don't want to miss anything, so your eyes scan huge sections in one go, lingering briefly on interesting looking jackets or strange titles. You will pick things up but get bored after the first few lines of blurb.

The Favouritist. You make a beeline for your favourite authors and quickly check that they haven't published a new book without you knowing. They never have. You then proceed to rearrange their titles on the shelf so that other shoppers are more likely to come across them.

The Janitor. A nice leisurely browse, tidying as you go. Booksellers of the world love people like you.

The Gambler. Pure pot luck. You pick up anything that comes to hand using whatever method works for you that day. You end up taking home a bunch of stuff you've never heard of just to see what it is like.

The Pigeonholer. You know what you like and like what you know. You head straight for your department of choice, never deviating or being swayed by multibuys or special offers. You are rarely surprised.

The Abramovitch. It is pay-day and you buy everything that looks remotely attractive or interesting and end up with a pile of books that you will struggle to fit on your shelves.

Breakfast in bed

This is the one thing no one minds being woken up early for and is the rare occasion when a continental breakfast isn't a disappointment.

Breaking the ice on a puddle

Once you reach about the age of ten you stop being magnetically attracted to rain puddles. No longer do you jump straight into them, wellies or not. No more do you risk the anger of your mum for getting your socks all wet. You are growing up and jumping in puddles is something you choose, albeit reluctantly, to leave behind.

A frozen puddle, however, is a different thing entirely. It is almost impossible for an adult to walk past one without testing it with their foot in the illicit hope of that beautiful and satisfying crack and the spider web of fractures as you break the surface. It is the sort of moment that fuels an otherwise grey day.

Bubble wrap

Happy birthday, bubble wrap! Bubble wrap was invented by Marc Chavannes and Alfred Fielding in 1957, making it fifty years old this year (unless you are reading this later than 2007, in which case I am a little surprised by this book's longevity). Technically, the term 'bubble wrap' is trademarked by the Sealed Air Corporation and to avoid any legal wrangling I should refer to it as 'air cellular cushioning material', but then you wouldn't have a clue what I was talking about.

Originally, the inventors were trying to come up with a new type of wallpaper but ended up with a versatile packing material. Little did they know at the time that they had actually created one of the most pleasurable and hypnotic stress-relieving devices known to man, which is, of course, the real reason for its inclusion in this volume. The Sealed Air Corporation seem to have a sense of humour about this aspect of their product and even have a personality test on their website, which determines the sort of person you are by examining the way in which you pop the bubbles. For example, an extroverted and self-motivated person tends to throw bubble wrap on the floor and stamp all over it. I prefer to pop them one at a time, which makes me pragmatic and self-assured, apparently.

Fascinating Fact

Bubble Wrap Appreciation Day is celebrated on 29 January every year, with events to mark the occasion including popping relay races and bubble wrap sculpture.

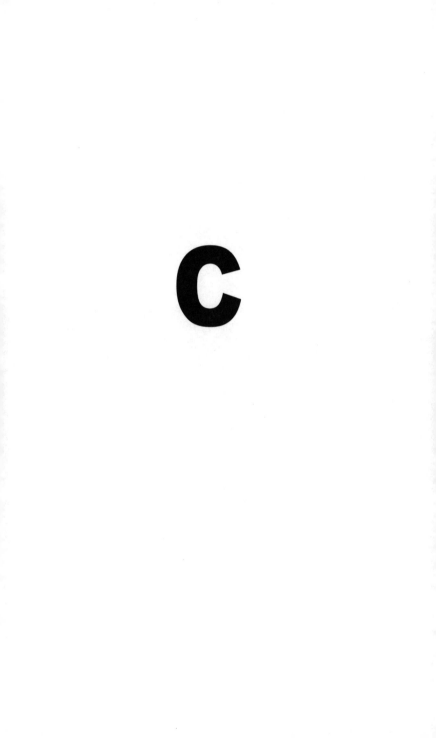

C

Cancelled meetings

You are snowed under at work, your inbox is full of unread emails and messages with red exclamation marks next to them, you haven't had time for lunch and you have a meeting you don't want to go to starting in half-an-hour.

Then a miracle happens. The boss's PA calls to tell you that, for reasons you are too giddy with excitement to hear, the meeting has been cancelled. Suddenly, your whole afternoon opens up before you like a beautiful summer field full of daisies. You feel like running barefoot through the car park and jumping for joy. Well, sort of.

Brian Cant

Brian Cant has managed to be a key performer in no fewer than five television shows that are now part of modern folklore: *Play School*, *Camberwick Green*, *Trumpton*, *Chigley* and *Play Away*. He was a fundamental, and fondly remembered, part of the early years of millions of children in the UK and around the world. He was, for most of the 1970s, the nation's storyteller.

A printer by training, Cant was playing around at amateur dramatics when he was offered a professional acting job and quit work the next day. After some time as a jobbing actor, he auditioned for a new BBC children's show called *Play School* and there began his stint in living rooms across the land.

Following an early period of heavily scripted shows, Cant got more involved in the production of *Play School* and ended up writing whole weeks of episodes. These were never live, as many people assume, but recorded a week ahead.

His appearances on *Play School* landed him some voiceover work for Gordon Murray and Freddie Phillips who were putting together an animated series for the BBC called *Camberwick Green*. This was such a success that he was asked back to do the same for *Trumpton* and *Chigley*. Recording his material in a converted broom cupboard, Cant didn't get to see the animations at the time and, to this day, has not seen every episode from the series.

Play Away evolved from *Play School* and was aimed at older children and recorded in front of a live studio audience. During his time on that show, he worked alongside actors such as Jeremy Irons and Tony Robinson, both of whom went on to enjoy success with an adult audience, but Cant will always be remembered for his work in children's television. Still acting today, he appears regularly on stage up and down the UK.

Personally I think it is about time that his significant achievements, and his place in the memories of millions, were recognised with an honour. Perhaps a knighthood is out of his reach, but an OBE or something like that wouldn't be too much to ask, would it?

Frank Capra movies

The word 'Capra-esque' is often used to describe a movie, or anything, really, which has a heart-warming, life-affirming and slightly magical quality. It came about because of director Frank Capra's tendency to produce films that ticked all those boxes, and many of his productions are considered all-time classics. His films include *Mr. Deeds Goes to Town* or *It Happened One Night*, which starred Clark Gable and Claudette Colbert and became the first film in history to win an Oscar for every major category.

Coming from a working-class background, Frank Capra was drawn to stories about the little man fighting against the odds, something epitomised by James Stewart's performances in *Mr. Smith Goes to Washington* and *It's a Wonderful Life*.

Capra himself was, by many accounts, not a particularly nice chap, but he was an excellent film director. He also knew how to pair up with talented people; many of his more successful films were penned by screenwriter Robert Riskin, a man whose vision is probably more aligned to the true meaning of Capra-esque.

Three Frank Capra movies appear on the American Film Institute's list of the 100 Greatest American Movies of all Time. These are *It's a Wonderful Life* (#11), *Mr. Smith Goes to Washington* (#29) and *It Happened One Night* (#35).

Cartoons

An artist draws an image on a sheet of paper. He then draws a slightly different image on another sheet. By quickly flicking between the two, he creates the illusion of movement. He has made a cartoon.

Take thousands of artists drawing millions of images over the past hundred years or so and you have a universe of animation that has brought joy, awe, wonder and amazement to everyone who has had the pleasure to witness them.

Cartoons unite us; they make us all smile; they are an experience we share with everyone else who has ever watched one. When my son laughs at Bugs and Daffy arguing over rabbit season/duck season, he is reliving the laughter I expressed when I was his age watching that very scene, which is precisely the same as my father before me.

Every now and then some morally outraged individual will complain about all the violence in animated cartoons. They will point to Jerry smashing Tom's face in with an iron, or Wile E. Coyote getting crushed by an anvil, and suggest that it is corrupting the minds of minors.

I say that they clearly didn't watch enough cartoons as a kid. If they did, they'd have a bloody sense of humour.

Children's paintings

On one hand, the critical and artistic one, children's paintings are basically crap. Of course they are. They are created by people with no artistic talent and with the most basic of materials. They tend to look nothing like their intended subject.

On the other hand, the emotional and creative one, they are little rectangles of pure imagination.

A blue strip of sky clings desperately to the top of the page. A monster with 13 legs and eyes hovering somewhere above its head explodes in a riot of colour. An incomprehensible mass of paint swirls together into impossible shapes. Go and see an infant school art display some time; they will be the greatest pictures you will ever see.

If you still aren't convinced that children's paintings are the most rewarding form of art we have, then ask yourself this. Why is it that all the great modern artists spend their adult lives trying to see the world as children again? If you want to paint as well as Picasso, you either have to be a genius …or five years old.

Chinese chips

Obviously it is a bit silly to order chips from a Chinese takeaway, but if you have ever done so, you will know that the Chinese have a secret magic recipe. Somehow their chips taste nicer than any others. I have no idea how they prepare them, and I have never thought to ask. Perhaps they cook them in a wok. Whatever it is they do, it elevates the chipped potato to a whole new level.

Church bells

I don't care what religion you are, the ringing of church bells on a sunny spring morning is a joy to the ears.

Close encounters with wildlife

Most wild animals steer well clear of us human beings. A very wise move, too – we have a tendency to kill them for food, sport, or out of sheer boredom. So when an otherwise shy creature happens across your path and doesn't instantly flee, it is a rare privilege.

Those brief seconds, silent and still, can seem timeless. As you make eye contact and, for a moment, you acknowledge each other's presence, it is as if you are communing with nature on an almost spiritual level. It is enough to humble even the most cynical of humans.

Clouds

Floating above our heads every day are the stuff of dreams and poetry. The most amazing sights in nature are just an upwards glance away.

Don't just take my word for it, here's someone who knows far more about it than me.

AN INTERVIEW WITH GAVIN PRETOR-PINNEY, FOUNDER OF THE CLOUD APPRECIATION SOCIETY.

What inspired you to start the Cloud Appreciation Society?

A few years back, a friend asked me to give a talk about clouds for her literary festival. She knew how enthusiastic I was about them and, of course, I said yes. But in the weeks before the event, I worried that no one would come along, since most people complain about clouds. It occurred to me that they might be more likely to come if I gave the talk an interesting name. So I called it 'The Inaugural Lecture of the Cloud Appreciation Society', even though no such society existed. When the talk was packed out, and everyone came up afterwards to ask how they could join, I figured that it was about time I started a society for real.

How many members do you have?
There are currently 7,700 members in 42 different countries, with more joining every day.

What are the benefits of membership as opposed to, I don't know, just looking up at the sky?
There are no particular benefits. We have yet to negotiate with airlines for members to have priority booking of window seats. But when you spend £3 to become a member, you get a badge and a certificate with your name and membership number on it. This states that you will 'pledge to persuade all who'll listen of the wonder and beauty of clouds'. Of course, you don't need to be a member to look up and enjoy clouds. They are there for anyone to enjoy. They belong to everyone and no one. It is about time someone stood up for clouds. It's just about that, really.

Any famous cloudspotters among your number, or is that a secret?
I have the utmost respect for the privacy of our members. Still, I can divulge that membership includes a celebrity chef, a musician/conceptual artist who had a number one hit single, and a husband-and-wife TV presenter duo.

What is it about clouds that you like so much?
I like the way they bring variety and drama to our skies. Life would be dull if we had to look up at monotonous blue skies day after day. Clouds are precious precisely because they are so transient: every cloudscape is

unique, and clouds generally are useful metaphors for life down on earth (just one of the reasons for their great credentials as subjects for poetry and art). Put simply: clouds are for dreamers and their contemplation benefits the soul. A few minutes looking up each day to let your mind float along with the clouds is the best form of meditation I know. It helps elevate you above earthly concerns – and saves on psychoanalysis bills.

What is your all-time favourite cloud?

It is either the pileus cloud or the lenticular cloud. A pileus is like a cloud haircut. It looks like a blow-dried bouffant, and sometimes forms on top of the puffy, cauliflower-like summit of a large cumulus cloud. It only lasts a few minutes, before the cumulus grows up through it. It therefore embodies the transitory, ephemeral nature of clouds. A lenticular cloud tends to form in hilly or mountainous regions. It looks like a flying saucer. Unlike most clouds that blow along in the wind, the lenticular formation hovers, more or less stationary, in a brisk breeze. One of the joys of cloudspotting is finding shapes, so this UFO-shaped cloud is a winner.

Cloudspotters: anoraks or poets?

Both. And that's the beauty of it.

Do you think people who appreciate clouds have a more optimistic outlook on life?

Yes. What could be more optimistic than finding profound beauty in the everyday? Let others find clouds mundane; let them spend fifty weeks of the year wishing they were on holiday somewhere else where the sky is always blue. If a dramatic display of altocumulus undulatus, cast in the warm light of the setting sun, appeared only once in a generation, it would become a legend. I don't think the fact that it happens on a weekly basis makes it any less remarkable.

(The Cloud Appreciation Society can be found online at www.cloudappreciationsociety.org. Gavin Pretor-Pinney is the author of The Cloudspotters' Guide, published by Sceptre.)

Columbo

Peter Falk's portrayal of the seemingly hapless LAPD homicide detective Lieutenant Columbo has become one of the most popular character performances in television history. With its genre-breaking format – the audience knew the identity of the killer from the outset – the show became hugely popular during the 1970s although the pilot episode was shot as far back as 1968. In fact, the character of Columbo dates from much earlier, having appeared in a one-off TV drama in 1960, written by creators Richard Levinson and William Link. In that live broadcast, Columbo was played by Bert Freed.

Although it had a unique approach to the cop show format, the makers of *Columbo* were not averse to the world of cliché and the programme built up its own repertoire over the years, much to the delight of fans and aficionados.

Enthusiasts revel in hearing Lt Columbo utter his catchphrases, 'just one more thing', or 'about that alibi of yours', watching him trying to find somewhere to stub out his cigar or parking his battered old Peugeot really badly.

The original '70s series featured a cornucopia of special guest stars including William Shatner, Robert Culp, Johnny Cash and Leonard Nimoy, but was a breeding ground for significant talent behind the screens as well – John Cassavetes, Jonathan Demme and Stephen Spielberg all directed episodes.

Now a staple of weekday afternoon television, *Columbo* continues to find new audiences every year and its appeal looks likely to go on for many more years to come.

FASCINATING FACT

Despite the protests of Columbo's star and creators, NBC produced a show called *Mrs. Columbo* in 1979. It featured the crimestopping adventures of the lieutenant's supposed wife and starred Kate Mulgrew who later went on to captain the USS Enterprise in *Star Trek: Voyager*. Unsurprisingly, it was cancelled after one season.

Constellations

If clouds are the poetry, then constellations are definitely the stories of the sky. They are thought to have been created by farmers in ancient times in order to more easily determine the seasons. They imagined shapes and characters within the star formations and some historians believe that these were the genesis of many ancient myths; by telling stories around these characters, they were better able to remember them and pass them down the generations.

Modern astronomy has changed the original formations somewhat, so that now every star in the sky is in exactly one constellation. There are 88 official constellations in the night sky.

Cracking a boiled egg

I suppose this falls into the same category as frozen puddles. Taking a spoon and giving a boiled egg a good beating is an intensely satisfying feeling. Not so severing the top with a knife; this is simply wrong and somewhat alarming. People who adopt that latter method are probably to be avoided.

A great practical joke when you are a child is to finish eating a boiled egg and then turn it upside down, trying to convince some unsuspecting victim (usually your dad) that it is indeed a nice, fresh new one. Actually, you don't have to be a kid at all to enjoy this. I am going to give it a go next time (and I am willing to bet that you do, too).

Cream teas

Every nation is rightly proud of its national dish but, for some reason, the English can never seem to decide what it is. Fish and chips was long held to be the meal in question, but then someone would pipe up and argue the toss for steak and kidney pie. In more recent years it has been claimed that curry is now the national dish, but this is clearly nonsense. I mean, curry is lovely and a very welcome addition to the national menu, but we really should make an effort to have one stand-out meal that isn't imported.

I would like to put forward the case for cream teas. A nice scone (fruit or plain) with a pot of jam and lashings of clotted cream. It is quintessentially English in the same way as haggis (or the deep-fried Mars bar) is Scottish and, I don't know, leeks I suppose are Welsh.

Historians in Tavistock, West Devon, believe that they have discovered the origins of the cream tea. Apparently, after the Vikings had plundered the Benedictine abbey there in AD 997, the monks relied on local workers to help them rebuild it. To thank the men, the monks fed them with bread, clotted cream and strawberry jam. The meal proved so popular that they continued to serve it to passing travellers and the cream tea was born.

Crumpets

I am writing these entries in strict alphabetical order, which means that I am now rather hungry. I could just go a bit of crumpet.

The crumpet has the double honour of being delicious toasted and also the cause of much innuendo in *Carry On* films.

There are times when only a hot crumpet dripping with melted butter will do, and it is in honour of these times that crumpets find themselves in this celebration of all things wonderful.

Danish pastries

Ahh, the breakfast of champions. Whenever I start the day with a Danish pastry, I raise my mug of tea to toast the good people of Denmark. Although, apparently, I should really be toasting Austrians and Americans as well. In all likelihood, what we know today as 'a Danish' was created in Vienna and made its way to Denmark, and other countries in northern Europe, by some sort of pastry osmosis.

Its real rise to fame was when it hit the shores of the US, which it did with great fanfare and huge success. A Danish baker and self-proclaimed '*patisserie-savant*' by the name of L.C. Klitteng came to New York towards the end of the nineteenth century, at the invitation of Broadway restaurateur, Herman Gertner. Between them they managed to convert the nation to the wonders of the Danish. To do so, they had to battle against the well-established French pastries, which were popular with the moneyed classes at the time. What ensued was nothing short of a propaganda war, albeit a reasonably friendly, and not to say tasty, one.

In newspaper ads and features across several years, the two men extolled the virtues of Danish pastries with cookery demonstrations and tasting sessions, particularly in and around New York. My favourite quote from one of these is as follows:

> *There is a difference between the Danish pastry and the French. The French pastry is eaten daintily and slowly, allowing each new discovery to sink in, and the flavors to blend one by one, until the effect of the whole is an Arabian dream of gastronomic thoughts. But with the Danish pastry – you just tuck a small morsel under the tongue, roll up the eyes, say 'Ah-h' as though there were a sky-rocket present, and it fades away and trickles down to the barbed-wire entanglements of the soul, a subtle something that clings like an opium eater's dream.*

Nigella Lawson, eat your heart out.

Ulises de la Cruz

Footballers are, on the whole, an over-paid, arrogant bunch, who think that the occasional appearance on *Children in Need* or *Comic Relief* makes them appear humble and worthy. I don't begrudge them their salaries, get what you can lads, and I know some do make a bit of an effort, but Ecuadorian footballer Ulises de la Cruz puts most of them to shame.

De la Cruz comes from the remote village of Piquiucho, three hours north of Ecuador's capital, Quito. The people of Piquiucho tended to live in ramshackle homes and the area was largely neglected by the government, but in recent years it has seen major rejuvenation.

Eleven miles of fresh water pipes have been laid to rid the village of the fungal infections spread for years by dirty water. A medical centre has opened with a full-time doctor, dentist and nurse. Education has been given a boost with a new roof for the local school, along with hundreds of books and a playground. Every morning, a hundred primary school children get breakfast and lunch provided for free, meals they may not have received otherwise. A new complex of homes, built to modern standards, is now under way.

Every single penny for this reconstruction and improvement has come from the pocket of Ulises de la Cruz. Currently playing for Reading in the Premiership, the footballer sends back ten per cent of his salary to fund the work of the foundation he set up. His mother, Edita, is in charge of making sure the money goes to the right causes.

Unlike many footballers, who count their success in trophies, adulation and sponsorships, de la Cruz equates his triumphs with what they can do for his home village:

> *The 2006 World Cup in Germany, when we reached the second round, was important because the success means I can finance a new sports and community centre, now under construction.*

Digital radio

It seems somewhat petty to hail the virtues of non-crackly radio just after the humbling tale of a selfless South American footballer, but alphabetical order tends to throw up these anomalies.

Of course, it isn't just the better reception that makes DAB digital radio so cool. Finally, we radio enthusiasts have the same sort of technology as television addicts have had for ages. We can now pause shows when the phone rings or we need the loo, we can access an EPG (electronic programme guide) to see what is coming up and scrolling text will tell us which song we are listening to or who is being interviewed. And if you are impressed by this, then just wait till you reach the exciting radio entry under 'I'.

Discovering water

There is a sudden rush of pleasure when you accidentally come across a stretch of water. You are out walking through the countryside and find a pond or stream that you weren't expecting, or better still a lake or river (although if it is the latter, then you really need to hone up your map reading skills). I was once walking the grounds of a stately home and found a waterfall, a good 30 feet tall, that I had no idea was going to be there. Magical.

Drawing pictures in steamed up windows

In years to come, archaeologists will unearth fragments of glass, breathe upon them in excitement and discover whole new languages – a world of mysterious hieroglyphs containing smiley faces and stick men.

Duck-billed platypus

Back to the Creationist argument. Many religious folk hold up the duck-billed platypus as proof that God exists. Only a supreme creator could come up with something so unique, they say. Atheists and those of a less fervent holy persuasion just look at the animal and laugh – if there is a God, then He was quite possibly off his face when He made that.

When the first platypus specimens were brought to England, they were viewed as a hoax. Here was an animal with a tail like a beaver but a duck bill for a nose; it laid eggs in the same way as a reptile or bird but suckled its young like a mammal. It went against all perceived notions of science at the time. It had to be a joke.

Although our knowledge has increased sufficiently since then to recognise that the platypus is actually a real animal, there are still huge gaps in our understanding of this odd-looking creature. Its mating habits are largely a mystery and we have no idea how long the gestation period lasts; the frontal shield at the top of the bill (the bit that rises up the forehead) is assumed to serve some purpose but zoologists have yet to work out what that may be. I hope the platypus keeps its secrets for a while yet.

FASCINATING FACT
The duck-billed platypus uses its tail in much the same way a camel does its hump. It is made up of fatty tissue which it uses as food in the lean winter months.

Dunking biscuits

Forget the cure for cancer or life in outer space, what scientists really need to be spending their time doing is working out the best method for dunking biscuits. And thank God they have.

Or should we? Whilst I rejoice in the idea that some boffin somewhere has wasted thousands of pounds of research grants calculating the precise formula for dunking perfection – the world needs such whimsy – it turns out that their findings are completely useless.

Get this; Dr Len Fisher from the University of Bristol ran not one, but two separate experiments into the Physics of Biscuit Dunking. The first was on method, the second on flavour. Here's what he found:

The ideal way to dunk a biscuit is to do so horizontally. By this, he means literally lowering the biscuit flat into liquid so that only the underneath is dunked. You remove it and quickly flip it upside down so that the undunked half supports the wet portion.

As for flavour, the best drink to dunk in is milk (hot or cold) and not tea or coffee. A good milk drink increases the flavour by a factor of ten. Apparently, he also worked out that dunking in lemonade reduces the flavour. No shit, Sherlock.

Both of these results are, as you are no doubt aware, utter tosh. Dunking biscuits is always to be done by dipping the biscuit vertically, immersing half of the solid into the hot liquid, and then rushing the whole thing to your mouth before it drops off. And the only drink worthy of dunking into is a nice cup of tea. You don't need a fancy degree and a white coat to work that out.

eBay

eBay is wonderful for two simple reasons.

1. If there is something you have always wanted to get hold of, even if it is extremely rare or obscure, you will find someone selling it on eBay.
2. No matter how crap or apparently worthless the piece of junk you have lying around, you will find someone to buy it on eBay.

eglus

A little as five years ago, keeping chickens was something people did in the countryside. They were a rare sight in cities and urban areas. That was, until four graduates from the Royal College of Art in London created the eglu.

An eglu is a plastic pod and run designed to enable people to keep chickens in even the smallest of suburban gardens. Looking like a cross between a Lego brick and an iMac screen, it comes in a variety of bright colours and has bought the joy of chickens to thousands of people who would otherwise never have considered it an option.

Omlet, the company behind the eglu phenomenon, believes that their little creation is actively changing the lives of its owners. 90 per cent of their orders come from people who have never kept livestock before, and 66 per cent claim to have become more self-sufficient in other areas since their eglu arrived.

The company have recently branched out into futuristic rabbit and guinea pig hutches and are going from strength to strength, bringing their green and pleasant philosophy to the greyer areas of the nation.

JOHANNES PAUL FOUNDED OMLET ALONGSIDE JAMES TUTHILL, SIMON NICHOLLS AND WILLIAM WINDHAM. I ASKED HIM A FEW QUESTIONS ABOUT THEIR INSPIRED INVENTION.

Where on earth did the idea for the eglu come from?

It's funny, people often say 'damn, I wish I'd thought of that' when they first see the eglu but when we were originally toying with the idea at the Royal College of Art, everyone kept saying how daft it was! James had the original brainwave during our degree in Industrial Design. He was trying to think of a final year project and mentioned that his mum had suggested designing a chicken house that was easy to clean, secure against foxes and looked good in the garden. Simon, Will and I got the potential of the concept straight away and we all decided to take the project on after we graduated – that was in 2003. We launched in May 2004 and it just took off; we had a lead article in the Easter edition of the Saturday *Times* announcing the eglu as the must-have item that would overtake the iPod and by Monday morning our inboxes were overflowing with emails from people from Canada to Japan wanting to know where they could get an eglu.

How does the finished version vary from the original concept?

I think like all really good design the production version is actually very close to the prototypes. This is because the original concept had a real clarity of purpose about it. The eglu broke new ground in the design of chicken houses or, more broadly speaking, pet products, which until then hadn't been considered part of the normal territory for designers to explore.

There is a strong community vibe on your website; is the eglu a lifestyle choice?

Putting an eglu and some chickens in your back garden is a real statement of intent. A lot of our customers are using the eglu as a way to dip a toe in self-sufficiency; one day they'd like to move to the country and have pigs and maybe even a cow, but for now the reality is children at school, work and other commitments, which make it tricky to move. The forum on our site, and we have now added a Wiki as well, are ways for eglu owners to exchange tips, skills and knowledge, not just on hens, but many other topics too. Many have gone on to add a vegetable patch, sign up for an allotment or even rear chickens to eat. Every now and again someone announces they have escaped to the country and everyone else celebrates – it's like a prison break!

How many eglus have been unleashed on the world so far?

Well, we have sold over 10,000 eglus across the UK now. In terms of chickens we estimate that's about 25,000 chickens laying around seven million eggs a year! We also launched the eglu in the States last year and that is starting to take off. There is even an eglu and two hens on Hawaii; I was seriously tempted to deliver that one personally.

Chickens, rabbits, guinea pigs – what's next for Omlet?

The eggciting thing is how much potential the eglu has given us for showing people that there is more to a garden than covering it in decking. The UK is unique as our towns and cities have an amazingly high percentage of houses with gardens. I think that the eglu has been so popular because people discover just how much they can achieve from even the smallest inner city plot. A couple of hens are as easy to look after as a goldfish and will provide a dozen eggs a week most of the year. Having vegetables growing in the garden, a compost heap and some chickens scratching about is so rewarding. Sure, it will require some time spent in the garden, but what's more important in life, eating well or catching the next episode of *EastEnders*?

Do you think people who keep chickens are happier as a result?

Yes! The thing about chickens is that as well as laying fantastic eggs, they are great pets too. Many a top executive who comes home stressed from the daily grind will go out to his back garden flock and after just a few moments in the company of his hens, will realise that life boils down to the simple pleasures of collecting a fresh egg in the morning and cooking it for breakfast. Hens are great for putting things in perspective.

(Omlet and their many pet houses can be found at www.omlet.co.uk.)

Extra hour in bed when the clocks go back

Obviously it isn't compulsory to stay in bed for the extra hour. Some people like to wake up as normal and make the most of the additional time. If you are one of those people, then I salute and applaud you, but could you please keep the noise down?

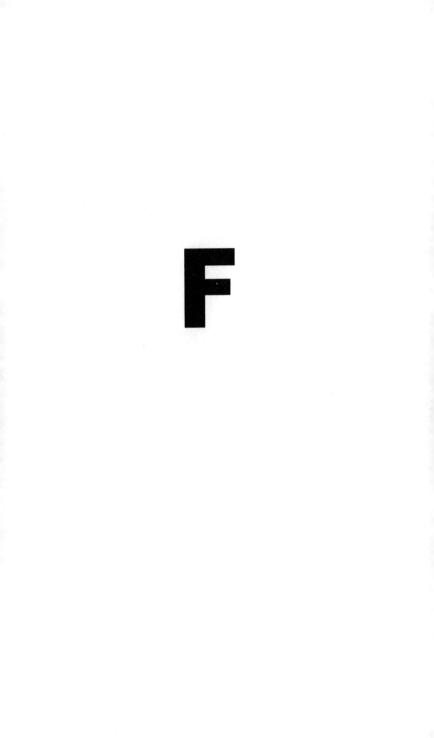

F

Falling in love

Now, I don't want to get all twee and slushy on you, and I promise not to linger on this one, but it would be remiss of me to ignore it. Falling in love is one of the most inspiring, life-affirming, empowering events we can experience. For some of us, it happens just once in our lifetime, for others it seems to occur a couple of times a day. No matter the whys and wherefores, when it does happen it is a thing to celebrate. As I write this, I am looking across at the woman I love and I find myself humbled and grateful. She makes me feel like I could move mountains. Not that I will; that would be foolish. I might just pop over and give her a kiss instead.

Fat Duck menu

In his small restaurant in Bray, a village in Berkshire that doesn't appear to have any pavements, chef Heston Blumenthal has created the most unusual menu on the planet. Whether it be snail porridge, or his green tea mousse cooked in liquid nitrogen, the dishes are inspirational and slightly mad. Eating them is unforgettable and, I am delighted to report, unlike many posh restaurants, no one at the Fat Duck takes themselves remotely seriously. The waiters smile throughout, some of the dishes are intended to make you laugh and half the pleasure is in watching other diners tuck into the bizarre concoctions you yourself have just tried. Sardines on toast ice cream, anyone?

Favourite shirt

We've all got one. Some moth-eaten old T-shirt or baggy button-down, which has become like an old friend. It is comforting to wear and has probably stuck with you longer than most of your friends. It becomes more threadbare with each wash and it probably isn't fit to be worn outside the house, but for those cold winter nights in front of the telly or curled up in the armchair with a good book, there is nothing better.

Field of Dreams

Not only does this feature film reduce most grown men to tears, they are quite happy to admit to it afterwards. On first glance, a movie starring Kevin Costner that features lots of baseball does not appear to be a recipe for a classic, but you will find *Field of Dreams* on most lists of the greatest films ever.

Farmer Ray Kinsella ploughs through his cornfield when he sees a vision of a baseball diamond and a voice telling him, 'If you build it, he will come.' His neighbours think him mad, but after a long wait the pitch is finally visited by the ghosts of dead baseball players. Ray is then sent on further quests that culminate with an emotional reunion with his dead father.

So what is it that makes *Field of Dreams* such a memorable movie? My theory is that it touches on a number of themes, each of which strikes a chord with a different member of its audience. You have a man following his dream, an emotional quest for lost heroes, the unifying power of sport, the magic of imagination and the one that gets you every time – what would you do if you had the chance to speak with the dearly departed? If you could speak with your dead father one more time, what would you say?

The real inspiration for the movie is the source material. W.P. Kinsella's novel, *Shoeless Joe* is every bit as magical as its screen adaptation, possibly more so, and introduces further elements to the story that did not make the final cut, such as Ray's identical twin brother coming to stay in the middle of the upheaval.

FASCINATING FACT
The owners of the land where the movie's baseball pitch was built have kept the diamond intact and visitors are free to come and play baseball there whenever they wish.

Finding something you thought you'd lost
The impact of this is amplified if you have genuinely given up hope of ever finding the item in question.

Fireworks
Fireworks were probably invented around 2,000 years ago in China. The popular myth is that a young cook accidentally mixed together sulphur, charcoal and saltpetre (all common in kitchens at the time) and things literally went bang. It wasn't until 1,000 years later, however, that the firecracker was invented, also in China, by a young monk from the Liu Yang region of Hunan Province. His name was Li Tian and his invention is celebrated on 18 April each

year by the offering of sacrifices. Liu Yang remains the centre of the world's firework manufacture to this day.

As many public information films have told us, fireworks can be dangerous things, but they also have the capacity to elicit collective gasps of awe from crowds of onlookers. They fill the sky with fire and colour and are used as a traditional celebration around the world. In the UK, their use tended to be restricted to Bonfire Night on 5 November, but the growing ethnic population means that we can enjoy displays all year round, most notably during the Hindu celebration of Diwali, the festival of light, in autumn. One cast-iron argument to use when people start spouting off about immigration is to point out that we get to see more fireworks now. That usually shuts them up.

First page of a new book

Books are bloody marvellous. They can be life-changing; they can inspire; they can anger and incite; they can move you; they can educate you; they can fill you with ambitions and dreams; they really can change the world. Which is why starting a new book brings with it such a tingle of anticipation. You just don't know which of the above effects, or any others, it may have. It could be the best book you will ever read. You could be a different person by the end of it. Starting a new book reminds you that life has endless potential.

First snow of winter

A few years ago, I was working in an office in a fairly dull area just outside London. It was an unremarkable day and the clock was ticking slowly. And then it started to snow, a real blizzard. Within a few minutes the car park was full of every Australian, New

Zealander, African and South African who worked in the building. They were outside with huge beaming grins and increasingly red noses, throwing snowballs and building snowmen. For many of them, this was the first time they had ever seen snow. It took me back to my childhood (I am sure it snowed more then) and reminded me of the excitement of the first snow of winter.

Fizzy feeling

That weird, slightly worrying, but somehow pleasurable sensation you get on the downstroke when swinging in a playground, or driving over a hump-backed bridge. My son calls it 'that fizzy feeling'.

The Flaming Lips

Most rock journalists agree that one of the best live bands in the world is the Flaming Lips. Their stage show is renowned for its inventiveness, sense of fun and just plain silliness. The show begins with thousands of giant balloons being launched upon the audience. These then spend the rest of the night being bounced all over the place, often into and onto the band members themselves. On their most recent tour, each performance was introduced by a town crier and the sides of the stage were flanked by a group of Santas on one side and a herd of green aliens in mini-dresses on the other. Lead singer Wayne Coyne would then climb inside a giant hamster ball and surf across the audience while the rest of the band played an elongated introduction to the opening number. Once extricated from his ball, Coyne would periodically fire industrial-sized party poppers into the air, spraying confetti and streamers over the undulating crowd. All this with rock 'n' roll too!

The Flaming Lips are also notorious for their upbeat view on life, and irreverent distrust of authority. Songs such as *Do You Realise?* and *My Cosmic Autumn Rebellion* champion the rights of dreamers and idealists. They also do a mean version of *What a Wonderful World*.

Flickerbooks

Flickerbooks, also known as flip books or 'thumb cinema', are short books of images which, when flicked through quickly, give the illusion of movement. They are the simplest and most primitive of animations but are great fun to play with.

Flipping pancakes

One day a year, amateur cooks, professional chefs and children alike spend amusing minutes throwing pancakes up into the air in the vain hope that they will catch them again. The amount of pleasure gained from this activity is in direct proportion to the number of pancakes littering the floor by the end.

Food served on a tray

Any food tastes better when served on a tray. It doesn't matter what it is.

Free fudge

On Saturdays in some market towns, teenage girls dress up in period costume and stand outside fudge shops offering samples to tourists and locals. For them it is a mildly embarrassing weekend job, for us passers-by it is free fudge. Result.

Free hugs

One afternoon in 2004, at the Pitt Street Mall in Sydney, Australia, a young man walks up and down holding up a sign saying simply **FREE HUGS** in big black letters. After prolonged initial scepticism, he eventually persuades someone to give him a hug and than a chain reaction unfolds with dozens of complete strangers hugging him, and each other. The participants are eventually removed from the mall by security men, but they fight back with a petition and end up with 10,000 signatures demanding the right to free hugs.

The whole sequence of events was filmed by a video camera and then set to music. The resulting clip was uploaded onto YouTube and within weeks had been downloaded over ten million times. It became an Internet phenomenon and inspired similar campaigns throughout the world.

The individual who started it all, he goes by the pseudonym Juan Mann, has since set up a charity called Free Help, which tries to bring together people who need assistance for a variety of problems and those able to help for no charge.

The Free Hugs campaign shows how one man standing in the middle of a shopping mall with a piece of cardboard can spread his message around the world. To do my little bit, I will ask you to hug the next person you see. Go on.

Free museums

In early 2001, the UK government announced that it was going to scrap entrance fees to all national galleries and museums. Since then, it hasn't cost a penny to visit a whole host of attractions and collections, and attendances have shot up as a result. To give you an idea, entry to the Natural History Museum cost £9 in 2001, so we are talking about substantial subsidies to make this happen. Just sometimes, those in power do something that is genuinely for the good of all. This was one such occasion.

Globes

There is something suitably humbling about holding the whole world in your hands (cue campfire singalong). You become aware of the sheer magnitude of the earth we live on and the tiny part you play in it. And it is great fun to spin a globe, too.

Good Hair Days

We hear a great deal about Bad Hair Days but these are, thankfully, few and far between. It is their scarcity that ensures they are remarked upon. Which means that the majority of days must be Good Hair ones. We should stop and celebrate that once in a while, in our own small ways.

James Alexander Gordon

Some voices have a hypnotic effect on the listener; they are calming and reassuring. James Alexander Gordon has read out the football scores on the BBC for over thirty years. He can currently be heard every Saturday afternoon, just after five o'clock, on Radio Five Live's *Sports Report*.

Gordon's career as a broadcaster is quite remarkable given his childhood. He was adopted as a baby after his mother died giving birth to him and he contracted polio at just six months of age. Growing up in and out of hospital and being educated in special schools, he also had to contend with a speech impediment. When his father bought him a wireless, he would read along with the football scores and shipping forecast, developing his trademark style, the genesis of which he describes thus:

> *If Rangers had won I would feel happy for them so my voice would go up. If Celtic had lost I would feel sorry for them so my voice would drop. To me that seemed logical. In those days it was funereal when people read the football scores. So I thought I would make it more musical.*

He certainly does that.

Growing your own veg

You plant a seed.
You water it.
You keep it free of weeds and pests and beasties.
You nurture it.
It begins to grow.
You coax it along, willing it upwards.

Eventually, if you are lucky, it grows to maturity: a carrot or cucumber, a lettuce or onion.

Then comes the time to harvest. You reap what you have sown.

And then you eat it.
It tastes bloomin' marvellous.

Guessing quiz show answers correctly

'1934!'

'Norman Foster!'

'Bananas!'

'Magnesium!'

If you shout answers at the screen often enough and with confidence, sooner or later you will strike it lucky. It helps if you are not entirely random and try to stay within the general vicinity of the likely answer, but that isn't essential.

I tried it while watching a recent episode of *University Challenge*. I got more right than the scruffy looking bloke in the glasses second from the left. I felt like a genius.

Guildo on *Eurovision*

If you remember the 1998 *Eurovision Song Contest* at all, then it will be the sight of transsexual Israeli, Dana International, winning in a frenzy of sequins that sticks in the mind. You probably don't remember that the UK entry, Imaani, was only just pipped to the top spot by six points, and that would be fair enough – most people erase the losers from their memories as soon as they can. But there was one other performance that night that was worthy of note and it was a performance that many rank as the finest in the history of the competition.

Guildo Horn was representing Germany, a country not known for song contest success, nor its sense of humour for that matter. He appeared, sitting on the edge of the stage with straggly hair, a turquoise velour suit and puffy sleeves. His song started slowly, *Guildo Hat Euch Lieb!* (*Guildo Loves You All!*), and he sang straight to camera. But then the band struck up and Guildo sprang, as if electrified, across the stage, performing with such cheesy power that the whole studio audience were up and dancing. In true Iggy Pop style he launched himself into the crowd, greeting, embracing and kissing various onlookers before running back on stage in time to perform a cowbell solo. This was stupendous stuff, but Guildo was not finished yet. Spying a gantry to the side of the stage, he jumped upon it, climbing to its full height and completed his song hanging off the edge.

The crowd went wild. Terry Wogan was flummoxed. *Eurovision* had witnessed a legendary performance.

He finished seventh. Eight years later, a bunch of Finnish rockers dressed as Orcs romped home. Where is the justice?

Haiku

Haiku is a form of Japanese poetry that follows a strict structure but is intended to prompt an emotional response from the reader. Each haiku follows a 5–7–5 syllable structure. In the original Japanese it would usually be written as one line, but when translated into English it tends to be rendered into three.

The best definition of the motivation behind writing haiku can be found in *The Haiku Handbook* by William J. Higginson:

> *It is hard to tell you how I am feeling. Perhaps if I share with you the event that made me aware of these feelings, you will have similar feelings of your own.*

Traditional haiku would normally take nature as its subject, often with the poet observing a natural phenomenon of some kind. It would also feature a prominent grammatical break at the end of the first or second line. A good example is this haiku:

> *Furu ike ya*
> *kawazu tobikomu*
> *mizu no oto*

This was written by Basho, one of the most famous and revered haiku poets. He lived from 1644 to 1694 and began writing haiku at the age of 18. His work contains some of the most beautiful and thought-provoking poetry of any culture and the haiku above is one of the most famous in Japanese literature. It has been translated many times by a variety of translators but this version is by R.H. Blyth:

> *The old pond.*
> *A frog jumps in –*
> *the sound of the water.*

Haiku is no longer exclusive to Japanese and has been embraced worldwide. In the process it has shed some of its formalities so that nowadays most English language haiku simply follow the 5–7–5 structure but do not stick to the theme of nature or include the grammatical break.

> *I have to tell you –*
> *everything is not shit,*
> *so, it is just you.*

Hammocks

Lying on your back in a hammock, the sun filtering through the leaves of the tree above you, a gentle breeze rocking you slowly. An entire day can pass before you realise it.

Harold and Maude

A 20-something young man with an obsession for death: a woman pushing 80 with a thirst for life. They meet. They fall in love. They end up in bed together. You know, the typical rom-com.

Harold and Maude was released in 1971 and was a commercial flop but in the nearly forty years since then it has been elevated to classic status. The US Library of Congress selected it for preservation in 1997.

If you have never seen this film then get off your backside and do so soon, it will change the way you look at life. If you have, then you are probably smiling right now at the thought of it.

Having your child fall asleep in your arms

If this has ever happened to you, then you don't need me to tell you why it is in this book.

Helping lost tourists

They are just so disproportionately grateful when you do. It is as if you have saved the life of their firstborn or told them they have won the lottery. You can almost forgive them for walking too slowly in front of you with their day-glo rucksacks and taking ages to find the correct change when you are behind them in a queue to buy a newspaper.

I once told a man from Singapore which train station to get off at and he proceeded to take a photograph of me, note down my address and once he got back home he sent me a thank-you card and a copy of the photo. Obviously slightly nutty, but heart-warming nonetheless. A decade or so later, he probably still tells his neighbours about the lovely helpful man from England and shows them my photo on his mantelpiece. I wait to see if I am remembered in his will.

Honesty boxes

Tomato plants left outside someone's house; a charity bookcase at the train station; eggs for sale on a farm. Honesty boxes are left beside these, and many other such examples, in the expectation that you will pay for the items you take. The person selling the plants or books or eggs trusts you to leave the right money. Did you notice that word? Trust. Watching the news nowadays, you'd think there was no such thing, but all over the place people are trusting complete strangers to do the decent thing and pay for items even when there is no one there to see them do so. Warms your cockles, doesn't it?

Honey

Honey is a miraculous substance but we tend to take it for granted. Well, I would like to suggest that you take a few seconds to ponder quite how amazing it actually is. Here are some things you may not know about honey, and even if you do, they are worth reading again:

- It is the only foodstuff that doesn't go off. You can keep it forever. Pots of honey were found in Tutankhamen's tomb and were still edible.
- To make one pound of honey bees will have travelled over 50,000 miles and visited as many as two million flowers.
- A beekeeper in Somerset has perfected a system to get bees to make honey straight in the jars (I am not making this up).
- Honey changes flavour depending upon the flowers the bees visited to make it. The darker the honey, the stronger the flavour.
- The ancient Egyptians used to pay their taxes in honey.

- The Paris Opera House has a hive of bees in the roof and their honey is on sale in the foyer.
- Honey is the only food eaten by man that is made by insects.

The medicinal qualities of honey have been known for thousands of years. Professional singers still take honey to keep their throats healthy. It is also full of antioxidants and contains traces of a wide array of vitamins and minerals. Nature's sweetener is good for you.

Hotel breakfasts

Not the room service ones; they cost more and you get a finite amount. I am talking about the breakfast buffets in the restaurant. Typically, these comprise a range of fruit juices, yoghurt, cereals, muesli, fruit salad, croissants, Danish pastries, toast, cold cuts, bacon, sausages, beans, scrambled egg, hash browns, tomatoes, black pudding, mushrooms and tea or coffee. And here is the thing – you can eat as much as you want. Take a plate, fill it up, and go back time and time again. Go about the task properly and you won't need to eat again for a week.

Hourglasses

Watching time drain away, grain by grain, should probably be a depressing experience. But the thing about hourglasses, and the reason they are a wonderful metaphor for life, is that when the sand runs out you can turn them over and start all over again. Just don't forget to take your egg out of the pan or it will be over-cooked.

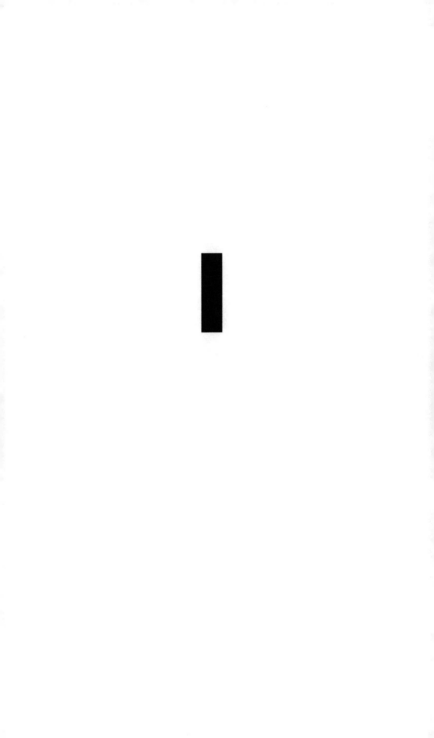

Ice cream

There are few problems or emotional crises that a tub of ice cream cannot fix. The rejuvenating properties of ice cream are technically, and medically, non-existent but, if that is the case, then why do we feel so much better after eating some?

The origins of ice cream are steeped in mystery and largely lost to time. Most of the great civilisations appear to have had their own versions of iced desserts and treats. The ancient Greeks served snow mixed with honey; the Persians would use ice to create sweet confections; the Emperor Nero had ice brought down from the mountains to freeze his fruit drinks; Alexander the Great was said to be fond of an early version of the dessert; the Indian sub-continent has been home to the dish kulfi for hundreds of years.

Modern mythology suggests that Marco Polo brought back the idea of ice cream from his visits to China and that is why Italy is so closely associated with the dish, but there is actually no evidence for this. In the UK, there are accounts of an iced pudding being prepared for Charles I by his chef. So impressed was the king that he paid the chef a huge salary to keep the recipe secret and only serve it at royal banquets. Again, this cannot be verified.

In all likelihood, numerous forms of iced dessert or sweet developed at different times in different places. As refrigeration became cheaper and more commonplace, we entered the modern era of ice cream, when it became a popular treat for all classes.

FASCINATING FACT

We have Margaret Thatcher to thank for Mr Whippy. The young Iron Lady was part of a research team that pioneered a way of increasing the amount of air in ice cream, thereby making it softer and able to be served by a pump machine straight into a cone.

Ice Hotel

Some creations are so fantastical, so unlikely, that you can't really believe they exist. The Ice Hotel is one such place. It should be the stuff of fairy tales – a vast building with many rooms, constructed completely of ice and snow – but it is a real place. At least it is for six months of the year; it melts away in the spring and is built again from scratch as winter approaches.

The company behind the original Ice Hotel, in Jukkasjärvi, northern Sweden, started out as a summer tourist operator offering various outdoor adventures for travellers. But in 1990 French artist Jannot Derit was invited to house an exhibition in a purpose-built igloo on the Torne River. It was a huge success, with visitors coming from all over the world to experience art in this unique setting. One group of tourists decided to stay overnight in the igloo gallery and the idea for an Ice Hotel was born.

Nowadays, the modern hotel continues to combine the concepts of art and snow, with sculptors and artists from around the world invited to design and create the many rooms. Visitors are welcome to walk through these rooms during the day to admire the work, but at night each room becomes a private sanctuary for its guests, lying on an ice bed covered in reindeer skins and snug inside a sleeping bag.

The architecture and features of the Ice Hotel change each year, although some elements remain constant. There is always an Ice Bar, mainly serving vodka because of its low freezing point, as well as an Ice Church at which hundreds of couples have been married. At times, the grounds have included an Ice Theatre, in which Shakespeare's *Macbeth* was performed in the Lapland language of Sami, and an Ice Cinema.

FASCINATING FACT

The roof of the Ice Hotel is strengthened with a mixture of snow and ice called, cleverly enough, 'snice'. The interior of the building stays at a constant −2 to −4°C at all times due to the insulation the snice provides.

Ice pops

A hot summer's day. A trip to the newsagents. Delving in the ice lolly freezer. You pull out a twelve-inch plastic tube full of neon orange frozen juice. As long as you can consume it without getting brain freeze, then you are in for a treat.

IKEA food

Unless you are under ten and still allowed to play in the bit with all the plastic balls, the cheap and plentiful grub is the one redeeming feature of a trip to IKEA. Even the most miserable of kids or begrudging of husbands can be enticed to endure the traffic queues and labyrinthine trek through flat-packed furniture with the promise of a plate of meatballs at the end of their visit.

I'm Sorry I Haven't a Clue

A new series of *I'm Sorry I Haven't a Clue* is greeted with such a cry of joy throughout the land that it probably registers on the Richter scale. This irreverent, slightly disorganised and repeatedly rather rude radio quiz show is a highlight of Radio 4's schedule and has built a huge international following.

It began in 1972 and the original line-up comprised Tim Brooke-Taylor, Jo Kendall, Graeme Garden and Bill Oddie on the teams. Barry Cryer and Humphrey Lyttelton would take turns to chair the show. Early on in its life, Cryer and Willie Rushton replaced Kendall and Oddie as panellists and Humph became the regular chairman. Since Rushton's death in 1997, a number of part-time panellists have sat in the spare seat, the most regular being comedian Jeremy Hardy.

The concept is really rather simple, with the teams engaging in a variety of parlour games, many of which have been slightly tweaked for comic effect. The show's popularity comes from the combined wit of the players as well as the winning comedy formula that has become routine over the thirty-five years or more of its life. So Humph will always introduce the teams with a not-very-thinly disguised insult and act vaguely disinterested in proceedings throughout; the scorer, Samantha, will be subject to some of the rudest and most blatant innuendo you will ever hear before the watershed; and pianist Colin Sell will be roundly ridiculed for his musical prowess. Most listeners are hooked after one show and the programme is now seen as a national treasure.

Innocent Smoothies packaging

Why more food manufacturers don't give you something interesting to read while you are sitting at the breakfast table is beyond me. Cereal packets could have short stories or, wait for it, serialised novels on the back. Sauce labels could easily sneak in a haiku or two. So, full marks and a round of applause to the nice people at Innocent, who plaster the packaging for their smoothie drinks with enough reading material to last a breakfast sitting.

So you may find instructions on how to turn an empty carton into a cress head, play spot the spoof ingredients (pickled onions and rubber ducks, anyone?) or you could always look at the base, to be told 'stop looking at my bottom'. Packaging with a sense of humour, designed to inspire a smirk.

Inspirational movies

The American Film Institute selected the 100 Most Inspiring Films of All Time back in 2006. The Top 10 were:

1. *It's a Wonderful Life* (1946)
2. *To Kill a Mockingbird* (1962)
3. *Schindler's List* (1993)
4. *Rocky* (1976)
5. *Mr. Smith Goes to Washington* (1939)
6. *E.T. The Extra-Terrestrial* (1982)

7. *The Grapes of Wrath* (1940)
8. *Breaking Away* (1979)
9. *Miracle on 34th Street* (1947)
10. *Saving Private Ryan* (1998)

Internet

You'd think the Internet was the sole cause of the world's ills, what with all the bad press it gets, but it is about time someone stood up for it. Any form of media is open to corruption and can be used as a negative force – look at books, newspapers, television over the course of history – but that does not make them inherently bad. No other technological advance has driven the size and scope of change and development that the Internet has generated; and nothing has moved so fast.

The Internet has empowered, informed, educated and inspired. As an accompaniment to our own minds and imaginations, it is second to none. The Internet is a good thing and our lives are better for it.

Internet community

One thing the Internet has brought back into many of our lives is a sense of community. It may be a shame that this huge, impersonal technological beast was the catalyst for this rediscovery, but that would be a petty quibble – it is nice to have it back.

Newsgroups, discussion forums, message boards, support sites, chat rooms, blogs, MySpace, social networking, there are a myriad of sites that invite our involvement. We are communicating with large groups of individuals on a daily basis and, on the whole, our lives are being enriched as a result.

On Amazon, other readers will tell you what they thought of the books they bought and you can see what other titles they like to read. On social networking sites, people are brought together based on their interests, the music they like, the places they visit etc. Support forums can be saviours. I recently had a problem with my laptop, posted a question on a computer support forum and six people quickly responded with suggestions and advice. Two of them kept helping out, offering detailed step-by-step instructions, until the issue was resolved. I have never met these people; I don't even know their real names. They had nothing to gain from helping out; it was just a nice thing to do.

Internet radio

Right now I can, if I so desire, listen to more or less any radio station currently broadcasting on the planet. I can find out what the travel is like in Brisbane, what news stories are making the headlines in Tokyo, check out the new music coming from New York, hear live opera from Venice, listen to real people tell real stories from anywhere on earth. With the advent of wireless Internet radio, the rest of the world really can enter my living room, or kitchen, or bathroom and life is all the more interesting for it.

Isle of Wight

It isn't so much that time has forgotten the Isle of Wight, more that time has *preserved* it. Described by many as 'England in miniature', a visit to the island is like a step back to the country of your childhood, no matter in which era you grew up.

The Isle of Wight is notable for many reasons, both current and historical. It is one of the last sanctuaries for the red squirrel in the UK; no grey squirrels exist on the island. It is a rich location for fossils and many intact dinosaur skeletons have been found over the years. Its distinct coloured sands can still be collected and displayed by eager children and adults alike. Its sense of community is like the England of yesteryear and there is something quite heartening about that.

It's a Wonderful Life

George Bailey, a young family man who has spent his life serving others, finds himself on a bridge outside his home town of Bedford Falls contemplating suicide. He faces financial ruin because of one silly mistake, something that isn't even his fault, and his world appears to be falling apart. Suddenly, he sees someone fall into the river and he jumps in to save them. That someone turns out to be Clarence, an angel (second class) sent to earth to help George in his hour of need. When George wishes he had never been born, Clarence makes that wish come true and takes him on a tour of Bedford Falls, a very different town without the influence of George Bailey.

So goes the basic premise of *It's a Wonderful Life*, one of the most treasured films in cinema history. To the outsider, or anyone unfamiliar with the film, it may seem a little trite or sentimental, but that would be a mistake. Frank Capra's classic movie is actually quite dark and sinister; many people forget the depths of despair that George Bailey is driven to, but it needs to be bleak and melancholy as that makes the final redemption all the more striking, all the more effective.

When first released in 1946 it was a commercial flop, losing money for the studio and the CIA considered it a subversive, pro-

Communist movie. As a result, it wallowed in obscurity for many years. Its enduring legacy is actually down to an administrative error. The movie was accidentally allowed to fall out of copyright, which meant that American TV stations could broadcast it for free and as a result it became a staple of Christmas viewing during the 1960s and '70s, elevating it to classic status. It now ranks as No. 1 in the American Film Institute's list of Most Inspiring Films of All Time.

J

Japanese cool stuff

The rest of the world looks on in wonder at the weird, wonderful and just plain cool stuff that comes out of Japan. Whether it be computer electronics (it was the country that brought us Space Invaders and almost every other major computer game development since), or green tea-flavoured Kit Kats, robot dogs or manga, Japan churns out the most amazing things. We look on from afar, slightly amused but secretly quite jealous.

AN INTERVIEW WITH PETER PAYNE FROM J-LIST.COM, ONE OF THE BIGGEST ONLINE JAPANESE STORES.

Why do you think the Japanese make so much cool stuff?

I'm not sure what it is about Japan that makes it such a mysterious place, but it certainly is. One thing I like about the Japanese is that they're very meticulous, always doing incredibly minute, detailed things, from creating an anime statue to making very small machines.

Do you have a particular favourite item that you sell?

We have so many items it's hard to choose, but I like the 'wacky things from Japan' category of items that we offer. Basically, anything that's silly, like the split-toe tabi boots, called ninja boots since ninja used to wear them for balancing while invading a castle. Things like that are fun to sell since no one expects to find them on J-List. Other similar items include the 'Poop Hat' (a soft plush hat that's, well, supposed to look like poop) and the 'Girlfriend Knee Pillow', a place to lay your head down on when you're tired but don't have a girlfriend. Also, 'Oppai Ball', a soft, water-filled boob that's great for when you need something to squeeze.

And what are the most popular items on your site?

The kanji message t-shirts are popular, especially 'I'm looking for a Japanese Girlfriend'. We've recently licensed Domo-kun and the Domo-kun shirts are flying out the door, too. Another big item for us are the Japanese snacks; Japan-only flavours of Kit Kat (Sakura Kit Kat, Green Tea Kit Kat, etc.) are huge.

Even though you have been living in Japan for some time and make a living from Japanese merchandise, do you still come across something and find it really weird?

Weird stuff in Japan? Yes, of course, they can always surprise you. The other day we got in an ashtray that features the manneken pis, that peeing statue in Belgium. When you're done with your cigarette, press the button and he pees on your cigarette.

What do you think the rest of the world could learn from Japan and Japanese culture?
Oh, lots. Mainly, let's all live by the mantra 'World Peace Through Shared Popular Culture'. There's nothing that's in Japan that isn't being enjoyed outside of Japan too, and vice versa.

(J-List can be found online at www.jlist.com and Peter Payne blogs regularly on life in Japan at www. peterpayne.net.)

Chuck Jones

Some individuals have had more impact on popular culture than others. Some people have created art that has touched lives all over the planet. Some entertainers have made the whole world smile. Chuck Jones is one of the rare people to have managed all three.

Jones was an animator and cartoon director. His creations include Road Runner, Wile E. Coyote, Pepé le Pew and Marvin the Martian. He helped to bring to life, and was behind many of the finest moments of, Bugs Bunny, Daffy Duck, Elmer Fudd, Porky Pig, Tom and Jerry.

He didn't compose symphonies, he didn't save lives, he didn't write classic literature – he made cartoons, and bloody good ones too.

Journey home

The greatest journey on earth is not the Trans-Siberian Railway, or trekking across the Himalaya. Nor is it being pulled in a sled by huskies through the Arctic wastes, or to the Galapagos and its isles of wonder. The greatest journey on earth is the one that takes you home. Simple as that.

Juggling for more than five seconds for the first time

Juggling is a mystery to most and takes years to master properly. Learning to juggle is a series of disappointments to a soundtrack of thuds as beanbags drop to the floor. But every now and again the apprentice juggler gets past the first few throws and starts to build up a rhythm; before they know it five seconds have elapsed, then ten, then twenty. Before too long, the inevitable happens, but for those splendid moments beforehand, the sense of achievement is massive and a spirit of invincibility fills the air.

Jumping the queue

Legitimately, of course. You know what it is like. A trip to the supermarket for a loaf of bread or some loo roll and you are stuck in a winding queue for the till behind an old lady who appears to be doing her annual shop or stocking up for a nuclear attack. You start to think of ways you can make a sandwich without bread, or alternatives to toilet paper as you really cannot be bothered to wait so long and then the woman in front spies your paltry load and allows you in front of her. Soon, everyone else follows suit and, before you know it, you are pocketing your change and waving your thanks to everyone as you wend your merry way full of love for your fellow man (and woman).

Just a Minute

This is a very specific entry. *Just a Minute* is a long-running Radio 4 quiz show in which contestants have to speak for one minute on a subject without repetition, hesitation or deviation. Many celebrities, actors and comedians have played it over the years but the finest episodes of the show, and the ones that earn it a place in this book, would feature the same classic line-up. Kenneth Williams, Derek Nimmo, Clement Freud and Peter Jones would wax lyrical under the chairmanship of Nicholas Parsons, and hours of classic radio were the result. With three of them no longer with us, we shall never hear its like again.

Krtek the Mole

You need to be a certain age to remember Krtek, probably over 30, but if you are and you do, then those memories are fond and nostalgic. *Krtek the Mole* was a Czech animation created by Zdenek Miller. It began in 1956 and ran for well over 50 episodes across many years. It was broadcast in the UK during the mid-'70s and inhabited the 4.25 p.m. slot, just before *Jackanory*. The animations lacked any narrator, relying instead on music and sound effects as well as generic vocals (a little like Pingu), and the usual plots involved Krtek helping out his friends, coming to some grief and then finally saving the day.

The animations were notable for two main reasons. First, their distinctive eastern European style was unusual in the UK and they stood out as unique and inventive, often employing surreal imagery. Second, the poor mole would often break down in tears following the failure of some scheme or other and this would lead to thousands of children following suit. Watching *Krtek the Mole* episodes today is just as rewarding (the animation is timeless) but a little less emotional.

Landmark Trust

The Landmark Trust was founded in 1965 by Sir John and Lady Smith. Its remit is to rescue historic buildings, and those of particular architectural interest, that would otherwise be lost, demolished or condemned. Once a property has been restored to its original glory it is then let out for short breaks and holidays, thereby ensuring the funds for upkeep.

It is such a neat idea, and it works. Great buildings are preserved and holidaymakers get to stay in properties the like of which are rarely available to the public.

The Landmark Trust has a special place in my heart as much of this book was written while hidden away in a thirteenth-century farmhouse that would no longer be standing if it wasn't for their fine work.

Last day of term

No uniform and you can bring in a toy. Halcyon days.

Last page of a long book

Ideally we are talking well over 600 pages, perhaps pushing a thousand. Something epic, a tome that has taken weeks and months to complete. Think *The Iliad*, think *Ulysses*, think Proust. The sense of achievement, the depth of knowledge and poetry you have absorbed, the selfish pleasure at actually having completed it, is immense. You can keep your marathons and your cross-channel swims, give me *Don Quixote* any day.

Lego

Small, coloured plastic bricks that can be pieced together to make more or less anything. Their potential is limitless; they are the building blocks of imagination.

Lego was created by a Danish carpenter by the name of Ole Kirk Christiansen. He started making wooden toys in 1932 during the Great Depression and quickly found success, giving his company the name Lego (*leg godt* means 'play well' in Danish). When he experimented with plastic bricks during the 1940s, his new products were met with scepticism and it took some years of perseverance and several tweaks in design before they really took off.

The final brick design and manufacture was settled upon in 1963 and bricks from that era can still be used with modern sets more than forty years later. Ironically, this is one of the reasons for a decline in sales in recent times – the original bricks are simply so well made that they get passed down through the generations and families don't need to buy new sets. In these days of temporariness and the throwaway culture, this is worthy of note. Thankfully, Lego have managed to survive the odd sales wobble due to a whole new market in licensed and collectible models featuring series such as *Star Wars* and *Harry Potter*.

Lenticular stuff

When I was a child, I used to have a lenticular ruler. A 12-inch strip of flexible plastic with pictures of dinosaurs. When you moved it from side to side, the dinosaurs raised their heads, walked to the left, munched on some leaves or attached an unwitting victim. It would keep me amused for ages and it is a proven scientific fact* that males of all ages are magnetically attracted to anything that displays a lenticular effect. Technology has taken lenticular engineering to new heights and it isn't just rulers nowadays, oh no, you can get huge advertising billboards that appear to move as you walk past them. You can usually spot these from a distance due to the number of adult males moving repeatedly backwards and forwards in front of them.

The way lenticular images work is by splicing two or more pictures together and arranging them in sequence behind a screen of prisms (usually just shaped plastic). The prisms refract the light so that the viewer can only see one complete picture at a time, but as the object moves through the field of vision, the other images slowly appear and create an animation effect.

Letter writing

Sort through your post on any morning, throw out the junk mail, put the bills to one side, and what are you left with? Probably nothing. As little as ten years ago, your postman would have been delivering letters, not Boden catalogues.

---

*Of course it isn't, but I bet I'm right.

If you are unfamiliar with letters, they are a form of communication involving the written word. Normally, an individual would write down some thoughts and news onto sheets of paper using a pen, pop it into an envelope and send to a friend or relative, or anyone else they cared to correspond with. It was a bit like an email, only a bit slower.

I am a staunch defender of the Internet, as you will have read earlier (if you are tackling this book in order), but there is one big drawback: people hardly write letters any more. Finding a handwritten letter on your doormat is as rare as a four-leafed clover or your chances of spotting a red squirrel anywhere other than the Isle of Wight.

Email and instant messaging has made communication quicker and easier than ever before and has removed the need for letters at all in many cases. This is a real shame, as there are few pleasures more personal than writing a letter, or receiving one for that matter. We must all know at least one person who would appreciate a short note through the post; if we all wrote one after reading this entry, then we would be passing on a small piece of friendliness.

LibraryThing

Chances are that if you are reading this, you like books. Then allow me to introduce you to LibraryThing. LibraryThing is an online community that enables you to catalogue your book collection and then, if you wish, socialise with other users. The functionality is simple and you can get your books listed within seconds of starting. If you are bit of an anal collector, then this is a dream of a website.

But the fun doesn't stop there, far from it. Once you have a few books listed, the software starts beavering away on your behalf. It shows you other users who share your books; recommendations start to appear, suggesting books you might like based on the ones you own; rankings of books and authors that you don't have, but that people with similar libraries do, can direct you to new discoveries; reading groups and clubs are available for you to join; and you can send messages to fellow members. It is possible to lose yourself for hours and fall in love with your book collection all over again.

TIM SPALDING, FOUNDER OF LIBRARYTHING, TALKS ABOUT THE SITE AND THE ADDICTIVE NATURE OF CATALOGUING BOOKS.

Why did you start LibraryThing?
I was 'scratching my own itch' and the itch of people like me. I had been cataloguing my books for years, mostly in Filemaker. I knew others did too. I thought it would be fun to make such an application and, from the start, to make it pick up more than just Amazon's data. It was also a fun project while I figured out what I was really going to do. Freelancing wasn't paying the books. Then KABOOM!

How big is it now in terms of members and books?
Technically 170,000 members. But that's anyone who ever signed up. The core is more like 30 or 50k. We have 12 million books as of a few days ago. That's

something like 2.5 million unique 'titles', although that's a very wiggly concept.

And how has it developed from your initial concept?

At very first it was just a cataloguing application. There were minimal social features. But I noticed people using it socially – posting URLs of their catalogue on their blogs, and so forth. So I developed the social features. By 'social', incidentally, I don't mean 'MySpace-y'. Lots of social features on LibraryThing involve no actual social contact, like recommendations and browsing someone's library without sending them messages. And the crowd-cataloguing on LibraryThing is also social without involving the risk of online romance or anything.

Along the way, I picked up a passion for recommending algorithms, oddball statistics and open business relations (e.g. how we deal with swap sites).

Why do you think that books inspire such devotion and such a desire to catalogue them?

Interesting question, and not one with a single answer. Certainly, the 'social' aspects of LibraryThing have always been there. It's great to talk to someone who's reading the same book you are, whether you get that experience in college, in a book group or in one of those 'one book one city' programmes. And people who love books generally self-identify strongly around their reading tastes. In my case, for example, I think

Nabokov, Herodotus, M.I. Finley, and Paul Graham have as much to do with who I am now as, say, where I grew up. And showing this off is a way of telling people who you are, and reaching out to others like you. I, for one, like to have my books very much 'on view' so someone coming to my home can spot some shared book and start a conversation. Anyway, LibraryThing takes this social dimension and moves it online.

The 'urge to catalogue' is one I understand, but for me the considerations are largely practical. Some LibraryThing people are basically 'sorters'. I can't be bothered to keep my sock drawer in order (and consequently tend to wear different coloured socks). For me, cataloguing my books is all about remembering what I have, and the social fun having it online creates.

Who are the most popular authors among LibraryThing members?

Here are the top 20 by book count and user count, ordered by user count. The Zeitgeist [one of the site's community pages] has them by book count.

Author	Users	Books
J.K. Rowling	18,233	87,384
J.R.R. Tolkien	15,735	50,700
C. S. Lewis	13,208	49,535
George Orwell	12,648	22,238
Dan Brown	12,540	23,656
Jane Austen	11,553	29,439

Neil Gaiman	11,424	56,456
William Shakespeare	10,768	36,663
Douglas Adams	10,690	28,408
Stephen King	10,422	68,716
J.D. Salinger	9,608	15,422
Charles Dickens	9,484	24,833
John Steinbeck	8,814	18,460
F. Scott Fitzgerald	8,482	13,185
Margaret Atwood	7,883	19,347
Kurt Vonnegut	7,878	23,005
Harper Lee	7,736	8,496
Ray Bradbury	7,697	16,502
Aldous Huxley	7,484	10,945
Gabriel Garcia Marquez	7,374	13,746

And do you have a favourite obscure title?

In graduate school I read and enjoyed Donald Engels's *Alexander the Great and the Logistics of the Macedonian Army*, and it spurred a minor epiphany in how I approached Alexander and ancient history in general. I only met a few other people at Michigan who'd read it. Anyway, on LibraryThing there are now over fifty members who've read it – *http://www.librarything. com/work/44723*. That's what LibraryThing is best for. I mean, you can stroll into any café and find someone who's read Harry Potter.

What are your plans for the site?

Keep growing it. Expand it. Keep it open and cool and un-evil.

And, finally, do you have a favourite story from the LibraryThing community?

I'm blanking on a specific story, but just that there is such a community. Social software is mostly the social, not the software, and somehow we lucked into that part. I have members sending all LibraryThing employees gift-certificates for Christmas, and sending books and coming up with reading lists for my one-year old son. When we threw a barbecue at the office in Portland, we had one person drive up from Worcester and a couple from Providence!

(The LibraryThing website can be found, surprisingly enough at www.librarything.com.)

Licking the bowl

Mum has been baking a cake. She passes you the mixing bowl. The next ten minutes vanish in a blur of sticky fingers. Nowadays I tend to use a spoon; that is when my kids don't get there first.

Lie-ins

Our adult lives are busy ones, full of deadlines and appointments, people to see and places to go. As a wise philosopher once said,* life moves pretty fast, if we don't stop and look around once in a while, we might miss it. What better way to follow that advice than by an extra couple of hours under the duvet?

---

*Actually, it was Ferris Bueller.

The Story of the Little Mole who knew it was None of His Business

You may not be aware of this children's picture book but I urge you to check it out. It is a work of genius, and one with an important social message to bestow.

A mole surfaces from his burrow one morning only to have another animal crap right on top of his head. He doesn't see who did it, what with him being quite a short-sighted chap, so sets off on a quest to find the culprit. To each animal he comes across, he asks the same question, 'Did you do this on my head?', pointing to the poo, which remains firmly in place. One by one they deny the charge, proving their innocence by depositing their own pile of poo as evidence. Eventually, the mole turns to a couple of flies for help who identify it as the work of Basil, the butcher's dog. The mole then exacts revenge by clambering on top of the kennel and depositing his own mole-size turd onto the sleeping Basil's noggin.

Written by Werner Holzwarth and illustrated by Wolf Erlbruch, this heart-warming tale carries an important message for children: if someone shits on you, then it is only right that you should shit on them. Hang on, that's not very nice. Oh well, it is a really funny book.

London Underground map

Next time you are travelling by tube, take a few seconds to ponder the London Underground map. Just think about the complexity of the information it conveys, and how it does it so simply and effectively, while at the same time looking like something a five-year-old would draw with a crayon.

The underground railway was opened in London in 1863 and the very first map to plot its lines simply inset the detail into a normal geographical map of the area. The maps evolved over time as more lines and stations were opened, necessitating some kind of key, and as early as 1908 the bright colour coding of each line was already being used, although the map bore little resemblance to the one we use today. This basic format stayed in place for another 25 years until Harry Beck came along.

Beck was an electrical draughtsman who used his knowledge of circuit diagrams to put together a new map for the Underground system, something he did under his own initiative. The management were unsure about public reaction so, on its debut in 1933, the printed map requested feedback from travellers. The response was overwhelmingly positive and Beck's design formed the basis of all tube maps to come.

FASCINATING FACT

The River Thames is the only overground feature that appears on the London Underground map.

Look Left/Look Right signs

When you walk the pavements and cross the streets of London and other British cities, you will often see the words LOOK LEFT or LOOK RIGHT painted onto the road. You may well take these for granted, and who would blame you. But here's the thing – they don't do them anywhere else. Makes you proud, doesn't it?

Lost property statistics

These are both fascinating and amusing in equal measure. Following on with the London theme (we are on the letter L after all), here are some of the items that ended up at the Transport for London Lost Property Office in one twelve-month period:

24,084 bags (and their contents)
20,846 books
19,583 items of clothing
14,112 wallets and purses
10,614 mobile phones
7,505 sets of keys
7,026 umbrellas
6,118 pairs of glasses
5,718 items of jewellery
2,671 gloves (of which 474 were single gloves)
303 perishable items

All of which, one must assume, have their own stories behind them, but the stories I'd really like to know are those behind these missing items, found on the TfL system during the same year:

an exercise machine
14-foot boat
stuffed eagle
an urn with cremation ashes
sack of sultanas
wedding dress
park bench

briefcase containing £10,000
grandfather clock

and, yes, a kitchen sink.

Loud music in an empty house

It rocks!

Lower league football supporters

I pity Manchester United fans. And Chelsea fans, for that matter. What sad, unfulfilling lives they must lead, knowing that every lost match means an earful at work the next day and any season without some silverware is a catastrophe of epic proportions.

The real stars of football are fans of lower league clubs. Many support teams that have never won any trophies, ever. Let me repeat that – they-have-never-won-anything. My own team have only won a single trophy in their 100-year history and that was the 3rd Division (North) championship over half a century ago.

So why is being a fan of such a club so wonderful? Simple – because any minor achievement is a bloody miracle. Finishing in the top half of League Two is something to celebrate. Drawing a Premiership team in the third round of the FA Cup is our Wembley final. Supporting a lowly club gives you so much more potential for rapture. Perennial under-achievers celebrate with more gusto.

Lush

When a new branch opens, it makes stinky towns smell nice.

Making your own bread

You can take out all your frustrations and pent-up anger with a jolly good kneading and then revel in your own creativity when you tuck into a nice, warm slice of home-made bread. There are few pleasures more therapeutic and wholesome.

And now lazy people can simulate the same feelings too, by investing in a breadmaking machine, which will do all the work for you

Marbles

These are the jewels and gems of childhood. Genuine games of marbles (drawing a chalk circle on the pavement, etc.) are played rarely now but the appeal of owning marbles doesn't seem to have diminished. In fact, there are many adult marble collectors, with particularly rare examples fetching high prices.

Stephon Marbury

Modern sportsmen and women can earn more money from sponsorship deals than they could ever make from their day job alone. Anna Kournikova famously became the highest earning tennis player of her day, despite never winning a singles tournament during her entire career. Companies will pay successful sports stars millions of pounds to wear their shoes, or shirts, or sweatbands, in the hope that this will encourage the person in the street to spend a fortune on their brands.

The fact that we have all come to accept the above scenario makes the case of Stephon Marbury all the more remarkable. Marbury is a basketball player with the New York Knicks, nicknamed 'Starbury' since he was a boy growing up in Coney Island.

Conscious of the pressures inner-city children face to spend hundreds of dollars on the latest Nike or Reebok trainers worn by their idols, Marbury teamed up with an American clothes chain to promote his own range of Starbury items. His brand of shoes sells for $14.98, and is supported by a whole host of similar items at affordable prices. In today's materialistic world, this is a remarkable stance to take by one sportsman.

Meerkats

Meerkats are extremely sociable creatures. Their sense of community and desire to look after one another is a lesson to us all. Each member of the gang, or mob, has a function that helps the group as a whole. The most famous of these is the 'lookout', one meerkat who stands on its hind legs, surveying the horizon and skies for any sign of danger.

Moments before waking

Those brief seconds, just before you wake up properly, when your brain has yet to engage. You haven't got a single trouble or worry in the world.

Monkey

In the worlds before Monkey, primal chaos reigned ...

At 6 p.m. on Friday 16 November 1979, BBC Two broadcast an unknown Japanese television show that it had dubbed into English. It was to become the stuff of legend, which is apt given the source material.

Monkey (or *Saiyuki* in Japanese) was the tale of a Buddhist priest called Tripitaka who is sent on a pilgrimage to India to collect some holy scriptures. On his journey he picks up a ragtag coterie of helpers, a monkey king, a pig spirit and a sea monster, and together they make the dangerous journey, fighting off demons and helping villagers along the way. The premise was based on an ancient Eastern legend and the show actually stuck quite close to the original story.

The programme quickly became a hit in the UK (it had already been one of the highest rated programmes in Japan) and was the talk of the playground and workplace every Monday. For kids, the appeal was the pantomime violence and kung-fu moves, for grown-ups the same was true, but a few of them also noticed the underlying story as well.

Viewed now, and even at the time, *Monkey* is an odd concoction. The priest, Tripitaka, was portrayed as a man but was very obviously played by a woman. The voiceovers appeared to be taking the piss, but were actually based on the original scripts and were clearly performed with some affection. The huge helpings of Eastern mythology and Buddhist teachings were highly unusual for prime-time family viewing. It was an unlikely success, but a very big one.

The Japanese series ran for 52 episodes but ended after the second season, without the pilgrims ever reaching India. Only 39 of these shows were dubbed for broadcast in the UK.

Nearly 30 years on, the show is enjoying a new lease of life on satellite and cable channels as well as being released on DVD. These include the 13 'missing' episodes, which have now been tracked down and dubbed by the original UK cast.

... the nature of Monkey was irrepressible!

FASCINATING FACT

Masaaki Sakai, who played Monkey in the original series, had a second (and more successful) career as a popular lounge singer in Japan – their version of Engelbert Humperdink.

Mr Men

When Adam Hargreaves asked his father, Roger, what a tickle looked like, his dad drew a round orange chap in a blue hat with long, stretchy arms. That was back in 1971 and one of the most successful children's book series was born. The *Mr Men* books have sold over 100 million copies worldwide. Roger Hargreaves wrote and illustrated forty-three *Mr Men* and thirty *Little Miss* stories before his death in 1988. True connoisseurs of the series will remember fondly the TV version narrated by Arthur Lowe.

Naps

There is a period of your life, between the ages of five and thirty-five, when naps play no part in your daily routine. Outside of that they are little oases of calm that punctuate the day. I am looking forward to reaching my sixties so that I can have even more of them.

Nice biscuits

No book claiming to be a guide to all things nice would be complete without this titular biscuit. Named after the French city, they were seen as a posh treat for afternoon tea when they first appeared in the 1920s. Nice is not a brand name and consequently lots of different companies make them all over the world. The recipes can vary, but all feature coconut as a key ingredient, tend to have a sprinkling of sugar and, of course, have the word 'NICE' embossed on the top.

And, if I may be permitted, an aside on the word 'nice'. In my children's school there is a poster that shows the word being thrown into a dustbin. 'Nice' is banned from all composition on the grounds that it isn't descriptive enough. Many teachers share this view, my own editor's mum won't allow the word in the house and she is a teacher. Enough, I say. There is nothing wrong with the word nice, it doesn't deserve to be ostracised in this way. It has never hurt anyone. I submit the short essay below by way of protest:

> <u>What I Did On My Holiday</u>, by Steve Stack
> We drove to Nice in the south of France where we stopped off for a cup of tea and some Nice biscuits. We had a jolly nice time.
> THE END

Nice cup of tea and a sit down

Nothing quite beats it. After a long day at work, or a bracing walk, perhaps a particularly hectic period of vacuuming, maybe to celebrate finishing the crossword – plonking yourself down in an armchair with a cuppa and a biscuit is the only solution.

Non-iron shirts

Clearly invented by the patron saint of Monday mornings.

Northern Lights

The Northern Lights, or *Aurora Borealis* to give them their real name, are the greatest light show on earth – bright, swirling curtains of light and colour that can move and change at great speed. It is like the greatest firework display you can imagine multiplied by a hundred. They can be found towards the North and South Poles. The area close to the North Pole, inside the Arctic Circle, is far more densely populated than the South, which is why the Northern Lights are better known and more celebrated than the Southern Lights, or *Aurora Australis*.

They are caused by the magnetic fields surrounding the Earth. Just like the poles on a magnet, the Earth's magnetic attraction is greatest at each end. Charged particles in the atmosphere react to these fields and whizz around, bumping into gas atoms, which then give off light. This is happening at such a rate that we get to see some dazzling displays. The frequency and potency of the auroras depend on the strength of solar winds, but I am not even going to attempt to get into that.

FASCINATING FACT

The Northern Lights are hugely popular with Japanese tourists, who can account for as much as 90 per cent of all visitors in some notorious viewing locations. Japanese newlyweds are often to be found wandering off for some privacy when the lights kick in as it is believed to be lucky to conceive a child under the *Aurora Borealis*.

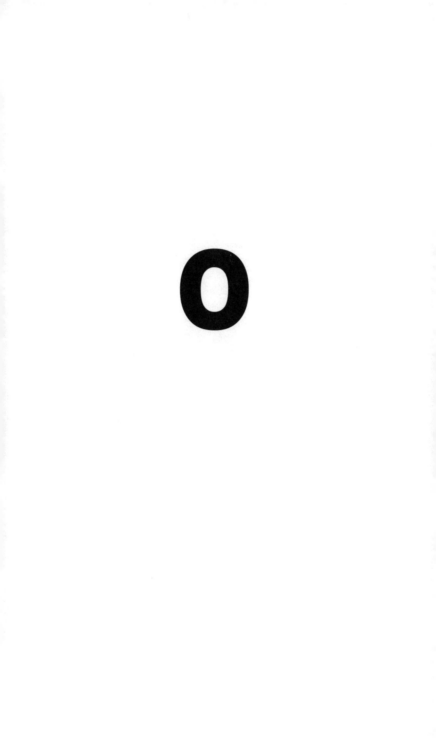

Old buildings

There is a certain reverence displayed by most people when they enter an old building, whether it be a church, town hall, residence or landmark. It is as if history has silenced them for a second. Certainly, it is hard not to ponder the dozens, if not hundreds and thousands, of lives that were lived within those walls. The births, marriages, deaths; the day-to-day drudgery, the moments of inspiration and joy. The space you occupy when inside an old building was, at one time, the centre of someone's life, a life lived long ago and possibly now forgotten. Although not quite; I like to think that the memories reside in the bricks, mortar and beams of these old places and it is the sense of this personal history that strikes us as we enter them.

One Man and His Dog

If you never saw this television programme (it has been off-air for almost a decade) then you might find the concept a little hard to believe – competitive sheepdog trials on the telly. Originally conceived to fulfil the BBC's countryside brief, it was firmly aimed at a rural audience but it ended up being hugely popular with city dwellers as well.

The format stayed pretty much the same across its twenty-three-year history. The presenters (Phil Drabble was the longest-running host) would interview farmers and shepherds while working their land, meeting their sheepdogs and finding out a bit about them. The action would then switch to the set, usually an agricultural show or country fair, where the contestants and their dogs would battle it out against each other in turn. The dogs had a pre-determined course to navigate, which would involve steering sheep around various obstacles, splitting the herd in two and finally coaxing them into a pen where the farmer would proudly slam the gate shut. Points were scored by a panel of judges for each part of the course and the winner of each show went through to the next round.

The beauty of the programme was the introduction of a dying country art to weekend television screens and the fact that even the uninitiated quickly became wrapped up in it. It was gripping stuff, while being comforting at the same time. The shepherds' meaningful whistles, shouts of 'Come by!' and 'Way lad', became part of the fabric of our lives and those who remember it do so very fondly.

Origami

There is a certain magic to taking a sheet of paper and turning it into a monkey, or a swan, or an elephant. If you know how to do it then you can create wonder in the eyes of your onlookers. It is an art form that has remained popular for hundreds of years and practically everyone has given it a go at one time or other, even if just to make a water bomb or that pinch-puzzle thing where you count out a sequence and then unfold it to reveal a forfeit.

Contrary to popular belief, origami did not originate in Japan. Although the name is of Japanese origin, it was not used to describe paper-folding in the West until the 1950s and it is likely that the European and Eastern traditions developed independently of one another. Indeed, in Spain there is a long history of making '*pajarita*' or paper birds, which pre-dates any major contact with Japan or China.

In modern origami, credit is given to the creator of a particular design (some have even patented their models) with their followers gaining pleasure from re-enacting the folding sequences to replicate the original. In Japan, it is really seen as an art form and has a wide following.

P

Paper aeroplanes

The poor man's origami. Not quite as artistic or beautiful but boy, can they fly! When you first teach a child to make paper aeroplanes and they see their creations soar across the room, they are stunned by the power of flight. With four or five folds you can span the heavens. A small piece of magic that all of us can create.

John Peel

Joni Mitchell once said something like 'you don't know what you've got till it's gone'. Those words have possibly never been more true than when the news came out that John Peel had died. He had been a part of the aural landscape for so long that his millions of listeners took him for granted; we assumed he would always be there and couldn't imagine radio without him. Well, now we do have radio without him and it is nowhere near as good.

John Robert Parker Ravenscroft was born in Cheshire in 1939. At boarding school one report mentioned his 'enthusiasm for unlistenable records', which turned out to be one of the most prescient comments in rock history. He spent the early '60s working as a DJ in America, starting out in Dallas playing popular hits but ending up in California where he aired a more eclectic and experimental selection.

He returned to the UK in 1967, only to leave these shores straight away for a stint as a pirate radio DJ, broadcasting from a ship in international waters. It was here that he finally became John Peel to avoid getting in trouble with the authorities under his real name.

When the pirate station was shut down, Peel found himself stumbling into a job with the BBC as one of the first Radio 1 DJs. He remained with that station, in one guise or another, right up to his death in 2004, and it was here that he became a legend. He pursued a unique course on the station, playing and championing new and exciting music, and could rightly claim to have helped launch the careers of numerous music legends. Every rock fan in the country remembers their stint as a Peel listener, and many never stopped.

His career took an unlikely turn when he began hosting Radio 4's *Home Truths* in 1998, a weekend magazine show that gave over the airwaves to real people with real stories. Peel's warm, but deadpan, delivery found a whole new audience.

When news of John Peel's death was announced, there was a wave of grief throughout the country, but unlike some less dignified outpourings, this one was tinged with gratitude. Millions of people not only wanted to say goodbye, but also 'thank you'. Roadside tributes were suspended from traffic signs, hundreds of bands dedicated live numbers to him, record stores blared out his favourite song, *Teenage Kicks* by The Undertones; a minute's noise was held, rather than a silence. It was spontaneous and it was heartfelt. Everyone seemed to think he was a nice bloke and we miss him.

Georges Perec

Georges Perec was an obscure experimental French writer and novelist whose surreal view of life has amused and inspired many who have discovered him. His most famous work, and one you will find in any good bookshop, is the novel *Life, a User's Manual*, in which the entire lives and histories of the residents of a Paris apartment block are frozen in time and recorded within the few seconds following the death of the landlord. Perec was a member of OuLiPo, a group of writers determined to introduce formal patterns to contemporary literature, borrowing rules and methods from disciplines such as chess and mathematics.

Perec loved to play with words and was particularly fond of palindromes and lipograms. Palindromes, as I am sure you are aware, are words or sentences that read the same forwards and backwards – 'Madam I'm Adam' is a famous example. Well, Perec created, in French, what is still the longest palindrome ever written, stretching to more than five thousand words. Lipograms are less common; they are texts in which one or more letters are not allowed to be used. His novel *La Disparition* was published in 1969 and concerns the disappearance of a man. It is a sort of literary whodunit, and the letter 'E' does not appear anywhere in the entire novel.

Georges Perec managed to create the most precise and clever literary constructions without ever once taking them too seriously. He brought a touch of the absurd to his work and no self-respecting home library should be without a few of his books. He also sported the finest beard and hair combination in modern literature.

FASCINATING FACT

When American writer Gilbert Adair translated Perec's lipogrammatic novel into English, he managed to do so without once using the letter 'E', possibly a greater feat than the original. Although a strict translation of the book's title would be '*The Disappearance*', Adair opted to go with '*A Void*' for obvious reasons.

Play-Doh

It is not unusual for adults to show nostalgia for some toy or game of their youth, but Play-Doh is probably the only example where grown-ups can get emotional by recalling its smell. Far from the most practical of building materials, it had to be stored in its airtight tubs or it would go hard, so you could never keep anything you made. It was invented accidentally by the McVicker brothers during the 1950s while they were trying to create a wallpaper cleaner. Over one billion pounds (in weight) of the stuff has been sold since.

FASCINATING FACT

To celebrate the fiftieth anniversary of Play-Doh in 2006 a limited edition fragrance was released, which replicated the familiar smell.

Playing sports against kids

At a recent visit to my son's school, a group of boys asked me to join in a game of football. Now, I am crap at football. I never played for a team at any level, I cannot do keepy-uppy for more than two or three goes; I have no football talent whatsoever. But these were a bunch of seven-year-olds and I only had my dignity to lose so I thought what the hell.

Surrounded by small boys, when the ball landed at my feet I was, by comparison, a giant. For a few brief minutes on that greenest of grasses I was a footballing genius. I was Pele. I was George Best. I was Garrincha, Eusebio and Maradona combined. I feinted left, I dummied to the right, my silky skills dribbled the ball from one end of the pitch to the other. I left the bodies of muddied schoolboys in my wake. I had only the keeper to beat. But then, in an act of utter selflessness, I passed the ball to the only member of my team who had managed to keep up with me, a tiny little chap who looked like he had stepped out of a Dickens novel. Never mind my personal glory I thought, here is your chance to be the hero of your classmates, Tiny Tim the ball is all yours. I timed the perfect knock back straight to his feet.

The little bastard missed, but the glory of those few moments has yet to leave me.

Popcorn

Not enough food is aurally satisfying in my opinion. The sizzle of bacon is nice. The whirr of a salad spinner can yield some pleasure. But when a pan of corn starts popping, that is the sound of little nuggets of joy.

Poppy Day

There are only a handful of people walking this earth who fought during the First World War and every year that passes leaves us with fewer survivors of the Second. In today's cynical and materialistic culture it perhaps wouldn't be surprising to see the younger generation ignore Remembrance Day, but given the numbers of teenagers and children who wear their poppies with pride, we can be safe in the knowledge that, even when all those brave men and women are gone, we will remember them.

Pre-dessert

And you thought an *amuse bouche* was good? Having stuffed your face full of entrées, hors-d'oeuvres, starters and main course, and while waiting for your pudding, along comes a mini-dessert that you weren't expecting. Heaven. The man who thought this up (and it was definitely a man) deserves a knighthood, or possibly a sainthood.

Pudding Club

In 1985 a group of friends, fed up with being offered Black Forest Gateau and defrosted cheesecake at the end of meals in restaurants, founded a society to bring back the great British pudding.

The Pudding Club is based at the Three Ways House Hotel in Mickleton, Gloucestershire and opens its doors to members and non-members alike. Diners will be treated to a very light main course, perhaps a small pasta dish or salmon with new potatoes, but then the real proceedings will commence. Seven gigantic puddings are paraded in front of the assembled guests, followed by vats of custard. The puds will vary from session to session but you can expect the traditional Sticky Toffee, Spotted Dick and

Syrup Sponge alongside less well-known dishes such as Sussex Pond.

Diners are allowed as many helpings as they want, but they must finish what is in their bowl before embarking upon a new course. It can be quite a struggle, but it is bloody well worth it.

Purple ones in tins of chocolates

A friend once told me that Cadbury had released a limited edition tin of chocolates that contained *only* the purple ones. If it did exist then it was as elusive as the Holy Grail because I never found one.

Pyramids

The single greatest engineering feat in the history of mankind.

Pyramid tea bags

The single greatest engineering feat in the history of tea and cake.

A quarter of ...

Your mum has given you 10p* for being good. You walk down the road to the corner shop. Standing on tiptoe you can just about see over the counter, and what awaits you is the sight of jars of sweets as far as the eye can see.

Humbugs, Mint Imperials, Tea Cakes, Sweet Tobacco, Chocolate Raisins, Aniseed Balls, Cough Candies, Sherbet Pips, Bon-bons, Liquorice Pipes, Pink Shrimps, Chocolate Mice, Sweet Peanuts, Fruit Gums, Wine Gums (if you had ID), Shoelaces, Butterscotch Creams, Rhubarb and Custard, Mojos, Black Jacks, Fruit Salads, Gobstoppers, Dolly Mixtures, Allsorts, Candy Cigarettes, Peanut Brittle, Coconut Mushrooms, Macaroons, Cola Cubes, Midget Gems, Liquorice Torpedoes, Pomfret Cakes, Sour Apples, Milk Bottles, Fizzy Coke Bottles, Cherry Lips, Floral Gums, Parma Violets (although no one ever bought those).

Coming across a selection like that nowadays is as rare as finding someone under the age of 90 who actually likes Parma Violets,

---

*Please adjust according to date of birth and/or inflation.

but I guess that makes it all the more special when you do. Every now and again, walking the streets of some small market town or village, a little shop will appear as you round a corner, looking somewhat like Emily's shop in *Bagpuss*, with a bay window and a squeaky hanging sign. You peer in through the glass and are transported back to the past.

Thankfully for us nostalgia addicts there are now online versions of our childhood sweetshops so that we can finish the job of rotting our teeth. They might not be as romantic and endearing as the originals but at least they still sell sweet tobacco.

MICHAEL PARKER, FOUNDER OF THE ONLINE SWEET SHOP A QUARTER OF, GETS ALL NOSTALGIC ABOUT THE CONFECTION OF HIS YOUTH.

How did A Quarter Of come about?

A Quarter Of started life in the Plough Inn, Winchmore Hill (Bucks) as my brother and I talked over a pint about the sweets we remembered as children. We remembered classics like Anglo Bubbly, Wham Bars, Shrimps and Sherbet Pips, and lamented their disappearance. I was, at the time, running my own marketing company and decided to look into whether they had disappeared and, to my utter delight, found that the vast majority of the sweets we remembered were still being made. Thinking what a shame it was that the disappearance of the corner sweetshop was causing these classic sweets to potentially disappear, I decided to attempt to recreate the sweetshop I remembered (The Chocolate Box, in Beaconsfield) on the web, and so A Quarter Of was born.

I was determined to create a shop that would bring back memories – not just a flogging shop – so enlisted the help of *Whizzer and Chips* cartoonist Colin Whittock, who created the heart and soul of the website, and who continues to create fantastic cartoons for the site to this day. A Quarter Of now has around six hundred sweets, from Sweet Tobacco to Gobstoppers, from Fizzy Cola Bottles to Space Dust, and loads more!

What are your Top 10 sellers?
1.   Flying Saucers
2.   Space Dust – Strawberry
3.   Sweet Tobacco
4.   White Chocolate Fish and Chips
5.   Foiled Ice Cups
6.   Sweet Peanuts
7.   Barratt's Candy Shrimps
8.   Chewing Nuts
9.   Milk Teeth
10. Anglo Bubbly Bubble Gum

Are there any classic confections of yesteryear that you are still trying to track down?
We have recently had a real coup and found two absolute classics that we've been searching for for AGES. One is Chelsea Whoppers (a kind of chocolatey, gooey fudge covered in chocolate powder), and the other is Crispets (little round chocolate nuggets with

bits of coconut and crispy rice) – we were getting so many emails asking for them that a couple of years ago we set ourselves the challenge of bringing them back. We eventually found they were still being made by an old-fashioned sweetmaker in Scotland, but we can't tell you who he is, as it's a closely-guarded secret! Other coups in the past have been Sweet Tobacco (coconut strands dipped in chocolate that look very much like tobacco) and Cherry Lips – which weren't easy to find either! Sadly, the sweets/bars we get asked for most now are impossible to get, as they are no longer manufactured: Aztec Bars, Texan Bars, Pacers and Spangles have been relegated to the sweet cemetery. Very sad ... although very occasionally there is light at the end of the tunnel: a couple of years ago, Nestlé started production of Texan bars for a limited period of six weeks – a Texan frenzy followed, and we sold 30,000 bars! It just goes to show the power of nostalgia... sweets really strike a chord with people.

What is the farthest-flung location you have shipped to?

We send sweets, mainly to homesick expats, all the time. We're constantly working to reduce international postage costs as we know that Brits living overseas often crave products that are classically British. We regularly send to Japan, New Zealand, Australia, South Africa and the Middle East.

Do you have a personal favourite item that you sell?

It's too difficult just to pick one! The one sweet that started the whole thing off was Anglo Bubbly, so we can't leave that one out, but Space Dust is definitely up there – who can forget pouring the stuff in, and letting it pop away... classic memories. Also, a really iconic sweet for me would be the brightly coloured plastic fruits filled with sherbet... very kitsch, very '70s. Lastly (I could go on for ages here!), I love our oversized sweets, like our Mahoosive Jumbo Gobstoppers (the size of a cricket ball – imagine how long it would take you to suck through that!), and our Mahoosive Marshmallow Cables (very, very long!).

How much do your staff spend on trips to the dentist each year?

We have an 'eat what you like while at work' policy, as we think everyone should know what they're working with (and there have to be some perks to working here!), but while it's quite common to see the guys out in the warehouse walking around with a lolly sticking out of their mouths, I'm happy to say that most of us abide by the 'everything in moderation' philosophy! Besides, I can honestly say that when you're surrounded by thousands of sweets all day every day, the desire dissipates somewhat. I never thought I'd say that, as I've got a very sweet tooth...

(You can order your own quarter of nostalgia from www.aquarterof.co.uk.)

Quiet carriages

So pissed off were travellers at having to sit next to people shouting 'I'm on a train!' down their mobile phones that train companies have created separate carriages from which such anti-social individuals are banned. So are people with iPods and their incessant 'chh chh chh chh' of songs from the hit parade that are loud enough to annoy but not quite sufficient for you to work out what they are bloody listening to. As all seasoned train passengers know, the commuting journey is an important place to catch up on sleep. Now, if they could just add snorers to the banned list...

Rain borders

I am not sure if these have an actual name; they are not weather fronts, these are something different. What I am talking about is that rare occurrence when you stand slap bang between an area of bright sunshine and a band of pouring rain.

I can remember one time when it was pissing down outside the front of my house but out the back it was so bright you needed to wear sunglasses. It lasted for several minutes and I kept running through one door and out the other in excitement. OK, so I was about ten but I am pretty sure I would do the same thing now.

On another occasion, I was waiting for a train on a bright summer's day when I noticed that the other end of the platform was dark. Not only was it dark but the rain was pouring down. Torrents of the stuff. I stood there amazed as this sheet of water made its way towards me. The other passengers were also watching and sharing the moment with each other. Our train arrived, but without exception we all waited until we were at least partially wet before jumping on board, smiling at each other in the secret knowledge of this meteorological event for the rest of the journey.

Rainbows

Richard **O**f **Y**ork **G**ave **B**attle **I**n **V**ain. Red, orange, yellow, green, blue, indigo and violet. A rainbow is caused when sunlight is dispersed through water, which is usually raindrops but they can occur at waterfalls as well. Acting like a prism, the drops of water refract the light from behind. The various wavelengths are bent at slightly different angles, which cause the optical effect for the viewer that we know as a rainbow.

But we don't care about all that. We just like spotting them. The pleasure of finding one in the sky does not seem to diminish with age, a bit like the excitement of hearing an ice cream van.

Precious Ramotswe

Mma Ramotswe is the heroine of *The No.1 Ladies' Detective Agency* series written by Alexander McCall Smith. Set in Botswana, the books have become a huge international success, primarily due to the gentle nature and homespun philosophy of their heroine. Precious Ramotswe rarely has to investigate anything too dangerous and tends to resolve marriage disputes or track down missing relatives, but she does so with an easy charm that wins over clients, criminals and readers alike.

Miss Read

Fans of an England of yesteryear: of village fêtes, leaving your door unlocked, walking country lanes and the local bobby cycling past could do worse than turn to the books of Miss Read. They capture a vision of England as it once was and shall never be again.

That is not to say that they are all chocolate-box portraits and idealised versions of country life, which they most certainly are not. Miss Read captured the *real* lives of country people, the bad with the good. So we see troubled marriages and genuine poverty, alcoholism and dark gossip alongside the more green and pleasant aspects of rural communities in the middle of the last century.

Miss Read was the pen name of Dora Saint who wrote over forty books, most of which were set in and around the fictional villages of Fairacre and Thrush Green. By setting much her work at the contemporary time of writing, and by having such a long career, Miss Read was able to record the lives of the village inhabitants as they changed across forty years. Her first novel, *Village School*, is narrated by Miss Clare, the new mistress of the Fairacre school and it is this character who relates most of the subsequent twenty novels set in that village, ending with *A Peaceful Retirement* in 1996, which was Saint's final book.

Reading in bed

Losing yourself in a good book has been a recurring theme of this one (and I haven't finished with the subject yet) and the location in which we choose to read is often as important as the book itself. Sleep experts claim that the brain needs time to wind down before we nod off and recommend that we do not use a computer screen or watch television for at least an hour before we go to bed. However, reading a book immediately before sleep is proven to improve the quality and benefit of the rest we get while sleeping. So, reading a book in bed is the healthy option.

Reading in the bath

If you are female, then there is a 60 per cent likelihood that you are reading this book in the bath (and may I take this opportunity to say how good you are looking?). Don't worry that the steam from the hot water will warp its pages, or that you are bound to drop it in at some point, the bath is a sanctuary for the cleaning of bodies and the reading of fine literature.

Reading on the loo

If you are a bloke there is a 99 per cent chance that this is where you are reading this book.

Sailing By

If you have ever been awake in the wee small hours and listening to Radio 4, then you will know this piece of music. *Sailing By* was composed in 1963 by Ronald Binge and is played at the end of domestic broadcast schedule each night, just before Radio 4 hands over to the World Service. It has lulled millions to sleep over the years, many of whom were up in arms when it was taken off air in 1993. The natural order of things was reinstated two years later when the powers-that-be saw sense and brought it back on to the schedule.

Satellite spotting

Watching the stars and constellations has occupied the time of every human who has ever walked the earth. But satellite spotting is, for hopefully obvious reasons, a relatively new pastime.

We can see satellites orbiting overhead because the sun reflects off them. This only takes place at dusk or just before dawn, when it is dark on the ground but there is still some light at the height of the orbiting satellite.

Not all the orbiting objects we can make out in the sky are satellites. Many of them are actually space debris, such as the rocket casings from many previous launches and also the International Space Station.

School trip gift shop purchases

At the end of every school trip, whether it be to a zoo, museum or other attraction, there is always the obligatory visit to the gift shop. These are a veritable treasure trove of worthless objects that are forgotten almost as soon as we get them home, but which crop up years later, laden with memories, when we sort through the stuff we have in the attic.

Sharpeners, erasers, huge pencils over a foot long, tiny pencils in a little holder, the aforementioned lenticular rulers, gonks, badges, stickers, something made out of a shell, snowglobes (more on these later), hats, notebooks, soft toys. All emblazoned with the logo of the attraction visited. Priceless artefacts one and all.

Dr Seuss

Theodor Seuss Geisel created over forty children's books under his pen name of Dr Seuss and is possibly the most widely read children's author of all time. With nearly every book he wrote being considered a classic – *The Cat in the Hat*, *How the Grinch Stole Christmas* and *Green Eggs and Ham* being perhaps the most famous of all – his surreal and irreverent style is as popular today as it was during his lifetime.

Geisel's work was a favourite of American school teachers during the 1950s and '60s as he wrote seemingly complex and detailed stories but with a small vocabulary of words, making them ideal for younger readers. He once accepted a bet that he couldn't write a book using only fifty words. The result was *Green Eggs and Ham*.

He often introduced a strong moral message in his work, but one that empowered children rather than preaching to them. His 1971 book *The Lorax* was a thinly-disguised case for environmentalism and *The Butter Battle Book* poked fun at the nuclear arms race.

FASCINATING FACT

During the Second World War, Theodor Geisel worked in the US film propaganda department alongside Frank Capra and Chuck Jones.

Seventies weather forecasts

In this modern age of computer graphics and virtual maps, it is hard for youngsters to believe that forecasts were once given using a cut-out map stuck to a wall with the weatherman sticking magnetic clouds around the country. It was fairly DIY and would look very amateur now, but here's the thing – we still knew what the weather was going to be like. It worked. It was a far more personal and (literally) hands-on way of communicating and I, for one, look back on those days with fondness.

Shipping forecast

Even if you do not understand a word of it, not one jot, the shipping forecast is nearly always essential listening and has developed a loyal following of non-seafarers, many of whom find its hypnotic repetition and mysterious content soothing.

It has a serious function though; it is an invaluable source of information for those taking to, or already on, the seas and provides current weather information as well as a forecast of conditions to come. It is broadcast four times a day on Radio 4 LW, with two of those broadcasts (00:48 and 05:20 hours) also appearing on FM.

A further appeal is the collection of names used to describe the various sea areas, working pretty much the way counties or provinces do on land. These are, in order: Viking, North Utsire, South Utsire, Forties, Cromarty, Forth, Tyne, Dogger, Fisher, German Bight, Humber, Thames, Dover, Wight, Portland, Plymouth, Biscay, FitzRoy, Sole, Lundy, Fastnet, Irish Sea, Shannon, Rockall, Malin, Hebrides, Bailey, Fair Isle, Faeroes, Southeast Iceland.

There is also an area known as Trafalgar, which is located off the coast of Spain, but this is only reported in the 00:48 broadcast.

Due to the importance of clarity and timing, the announcers reading the shipping forecast have to follow a strict sequence and the entire forecast is never more than 350 words long.

Skimming stones

Give anyone a stretch of water and a flat stone and they will do their best to send one skimming across the surface. There are few achievements greater than seeing your projectile bounce repeatedly along before plummeting to the depths to the sound of your cheers.

Although most people skim stones for fun, there are some who do it for glory. The World Stone Skimming Championships arrange contestants in lanes and have certain rules regarding stones and throwing. These are:

- The stone must be a natural formation.
- A maximum diameter of three inches is allowed.
- The stone must bounce at least three times.
- Each competitor gets five attempts.
- The stone that skims the furthest within its lane wins, regardless of the number of bounces.

Smallfilms

In a disused cow-shed on the outskirts of Canterbury, two men created worlds that have entertained children and adults for nearly fifty years.

Oliver Postgate and Peter Firmin had worked on a couple of early children's television shows (including live animation!) when they decided to start their own production company, which they called Smallfilms. From 1958 through to 1986 they made fifteen series, many of which are considered to be amongst the finest programmes of all time in the genre.

Their first widely broadcast series was *Ivor the Engine*, which ran from 1958–1963 on ITV and was shot in black and white. They remade these shows in 1975 in colour for the BBC. The *Sagas of Noggin the Nog* followed in 1959 and ran for five years. These followed the classic Smallfilms format of Postgate, with the help of an occasional actor, narrating the stories he had written and animating the characters that Firmin had drawn.

During this period of the early '60s they also made a number of programmes for ITV, such as *Pingwings* films and a 'live' programme, *The Dogwatch*, but these don't seem to have proved as enduring as the BBC shows.

Smallfilms' last black and white series for the BBC was *Pogles Wood*, the tales of small folk who lived in a tree. This ran till 1968 when it was replaced with *The Clangers*, their first foray into colour television. To create the Clangers' world, Firmin built a planet in his barn and populated it with aliens knitted by his wife Joan. Once again, Oliver animated the tales that he had scripted himself.

In 1973 there came along an old saggy cloth cat, which, nearly a quarter of a century later, was voted by BBC viewers as the greatest children's television programme of all time. *Bagpuss* started out as an idea of Firmin's. He thought of a retired army cat living in an Indian hospital where he told stories to the children. This proved too costly a concept to recreate so between them, Firmin and Postgate made an old shop, Emily's shop, and populated it with the characters we know and love.

Smallfilms carried on making children's programmes for more than a decade after *Bagpuss* finished in 1974, but the advent of faster-paced programming and a lack of imagination from producers meant they fell out of favour and fashion with the TV companies. How wrong they were – today *Bagpuss*, *The Clangers* and *Ivor the Engine* enjoy high ratings on satellite television and are masters of an extensive merchandising empire.

FASCINATING FACT

Bagpuss was originally intended to be a marmalade coloured cat but when the fabric came back from being dyed it ended up pink and white, so that is what they stuck with.

WHAT FOLLOWS IS A SHORT INTERVIEW WITH OLIVER POSTGATE, ONE-HALF OF THE SMALLFILMS PARTNERSHIP AND CO-CREATOR OF BAGPUSS, THE CLANGERS AND IVOR THE ENGINE.

Did you have any idea when you were making your programmes that they would still be being viewed nearly fifty years later?
Absolutely not. We had no time to think about such things. We needed the money.

Do any episodes stick out as particularly enjoyable to make?
Filming them was just a slog – enjoyment depended on the state of mind of the slogger.

How do you feel about the Smallfilms nostalgia so prevalent nowadays?
Delighted, but cautious. They are exceptional more for what they are not, than for what they are.

Have you been approached to remake any of your series?

Occasionally others have wanted to remake them, but 'with a more modern interpretation'. No thanks.

Bagpuss and his friends are now a range of popular merchandise. Do you have a favourite item, and is there anything you have said no to?

I, personally, do not have a favourite. But Peter and I are particular about the merchandise being consistent with the characters, and have occasionally turned versions down.

What are the future plans for the Smallfilms legacy?

I'm not sitting in that shed pushing Ivor along with a pin, frame by frame, again. But the films will continue to exist and our children may one day have plans for them.

(Oliver Postgate can occasionally be found commenting on matters of significantly more importance at his website www.oliverpostgate.co.uk and he also maintains a blog at www.newstatesman.com/blogs/oliver-postgate.)

Smiles

They don't hurt, even if they are contagious. Try one out right now. Great. Now, point it in someone else's direction. See? I bet you got one back in return. Or possibly you were arrested. If the latter, then feel free to use this book in your defence.

Snowglobes

There are objects that serve no practical function other than to amuse, and that surely is no bad thing. I think it is safe to say that snowglobes fall into that category.

The first snowglobes date from the early nineteenth century and were made from glass filled with water and bone chips. They were very fashionable with the upper classes during Victorian times and it wasn't until the 1950s that they became the common gift or souvenir item that they have remained to this day.

Sock football

Almost exclusively a bloke thing, but many is the FA Cup that has been won by the stunning volley of a rolled-up sock to the top right-hand corner of the wardrobe.

Someone else doing your ironing

Ironing's not that bad. Most people don't mind it. It can be a bit of a chore and when the basket is full to overflowing there is a sense of instability that pervades the house, but most people cope with it reasonably well.

So why is it such a blessed relief when someone else offers to do it for you? Your mother-in-law comes to stay and gets stuck into the pile, or a guest happily cracks on with your shirts once they've finished ironing their own. You don't even feel guilty, not for one second.

Sound jelly makes

Onomatopoeia is a wonderful concept but no word has been invented that can adequately describe the sound that jelly makes when it comes out of the mould, or when the first spoonful is dished out.

Thlurp!
Schlorb!
Floomp!

See, it can't be done.

Spinning coins

Instructions for spinning coins:

- Take a coin, any coin, but best to avoid 50p ones if you are a beginner.
- Stand it on edge vertically on a flat surface, placing your finger on top to support it.
- With your free hand, flick the side of the coin while, at the same time, releasing the steadying finger.
- With practice, and good timing, your coin should now be spinning merrily away and you need never be bored again.

Some coin spinners prefer an alternative method in which you hold the coin between the thumb and forefinger of each hand and give it a sharp twist and flick. This can work but has a lower success rate and is therefore not advisable for the beginner

Staying up late to finish a good book

Even though you have work in the morning, and despite knowing that you are going to be absolutely knackered if you stay up, you simply cannot put the book down and have to know how it ends. You can hear the church clock chime 1, and then 2, but still you plough on. When you turn the last page you are probably the only person awake in the street, but it was worth it.

The American author Ben Sherwood puts his email address in the 'About the Author' paragraph at the end of his novels. Some time ago he noticed that he received lots of emails from readers in the UK around 8 or 9p.m. his time, which would be about 1 or 2 in the morning in the UK. This struck him as odd, until he asked a couple of them and it turned out that they had been staying up late to finish his book and enjoyed it so much that, with everyone else asleep at home, they got straight on to the computer to tell him what they thought.

Sunday lunch

A proper Sunday lunch brings with it a certain amount of ceremony and tradition, often handed down through generations. The content, timing and process will differ from household to household but should always include:

a) some roast meat
b) a nice selection of veg
c) gravy, and lots of it

Optional extras include the accompanying condiments, which may be horseradish or mint sauce, mustards or jellies. Personally, I don't think a Sunday lunch qualifies as such without a Yorkshire pudding but I am aware that not all family chefs agree with me.

Sunday morning walks

Every person you walk past says good morning to you. It doesn't happen on any other day.

Sunny days in the garden

Preferably with a nice cool drink with lots of ice, the sound of insects buzzing around, a gentle breeze blowing through the leaves.

Sunrises

The dawn of a new day, and anything seems possible.

Sunsets

Even if we don't succeed, there is always tomorrow.

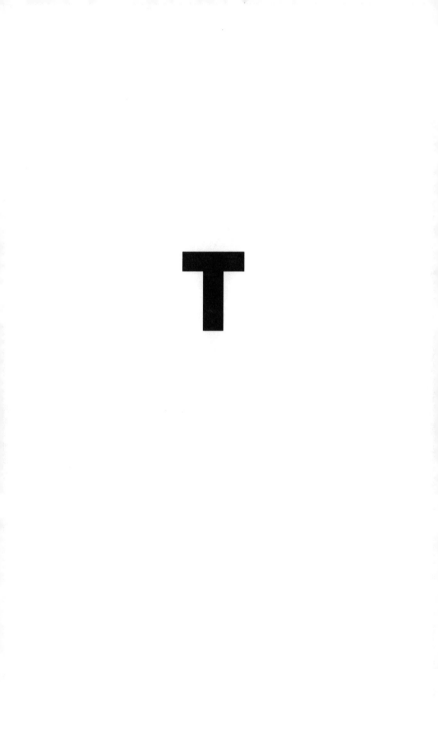

Taiwanese notebook slogans

Not just Taiwan actually; this is a trait of notebooks all over the Far East. Manufacturers of stationery in this part of the world like to put cheerful happy slogans on notepads, and they tend to do it in English. All of those listed below are actual slogans from notebooks and pads – I am not making any of them up.

Whatever you write on them is bound to be bright and happy.

The earth gave me dream and one lovely racoon, I know I was the luckiest man alive.

Hopes me to open the eye form the morning, goes to sleep until the evening, one all is all day fills happiness and the hope.

May the lucky star keep shining on you.

A smile walked with a friend contains only a hundred steps.

If you want, I'll be the wind for your stifling heart.

In this peaceful time I say your name, the wind answers and smile.

Owning this is one of my greatest enjoyments.

Wishing you a day that begins and ends on a delightful time.

The good mood is a vitamin pill for the soul.

There appears to be no commercial reason for doing this, they are just there. Beats a trip to Ryman's any day.

Treehouses
They are just cool. There isn't a child in the land who wouldn't want one and pretty much all of their parents would be up for it as well.

In Sweden there is now a treehouse hotel called the Woodpecker Hotel. It is the smallest of its kind in the world and is set 42½ feet above a public park in Vasteras, near Stockholm, in a large tree. It can sleep one couple at a time.

Trumptonshire trilogy
Gordon Murray created a stop-frame animation programme called *Camberwick Green* in 1966. It was broadcast as part of the *Watch with Mother* series before getting its own slot. It was followed in 1967 by *Trumpton* and in 1969 by *Chigley*. All three series were set in the county of Trumptonshire and often featured overlapping characters. It can be difficult to tell the three shows apart when looking back through the mists of time so here is a handy ready reckoner.

Camberwick Green

- Always started with a character rising up out of a music box. We would then follow that character through their day.
- Narrator Brian Cant would begin each episode with the line, 'Here is a box, a musical box, wound up and ready to play'.
- Regular characters included Windy Miller and the soldiers of Pippin Fort.
- In one episode, Windy gets pissed on cider and passes out beneath his windmill and the soldiers have to save the day.

Trumpton

- Each show started with the clock on the town hall and the words, 'Here is the clock, the Trumpton clock. Telling the time steadily, sensibly, never too quickly'.
- Most of the episodes were set in and around the market square.
- This is the one that featured the legendary fire brigade, Pugh, Pugh, Barney McGrew, Cuthbert, Dibble, Grub, under the auspices of Captain Flack.
- The firemen only ever attended one actual fire throughout all three series.

Chigley

- Featured Lord Belborough and his butler Brackett at Winkstead Hall.
- Included the song *Time Goes by When You're the Driver of a Train*.
- A regular location was the Creswell's biscuit factory.
- At the end of each episode the characters all got together for a dance.

Creator Gordon Murray famously destroyed the old sets and models from all three series on a bonfire in his garden. The only original that remains is one of the soldiers that Murray's daughter gave away as a gift.

U

Underwater swimming

Even if you can't swim above the water all that well, there is still pleasure to be had zooming around underneath like the Man from Atlantis.

Watching people swim underwater is also a curiously entertaining affair. There aren't as many of them around now but there used to be many public pools that had viewing areas set beneath the water level. So you could enjoy your vending machine snack while watching alien-like life forms perform a strange combination of ballet and drowning.

Unicycles

The bicycle for dreamers and optimists. A seemingly impossible thing to master but never to be taken seriously. Unicyclists are part clown, part Lance Armstrong.

Point to note: if you do fancy learning to unicycle and take your vehicle to a public park to practise, then every other person in the park will assume you already *can* unicycle. I mean, what sort of idiot would go out in public with that contraption if he wasn't able to ride it?

Yes, quite.

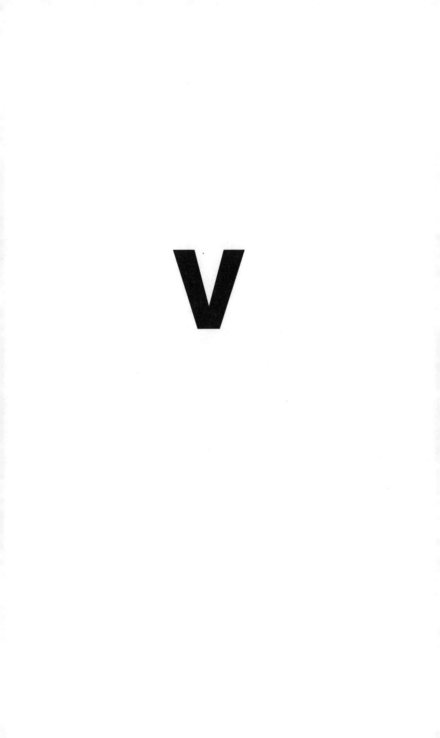

Velcro

Just for the sound it makes. When I get old I might end up thanking it for keeping my trousers up, but for now the sound will do.

Victory for the underdog

If you don't support either team in a football match, or if you don't care who wins the tennis final, then it always pays to support the underdog. There is so much more to gain. Absolutely no one expects them to win, including the players themselves, so everyone can dive into proceedings with a sense of abandon.

Ninety-nine times out of a hundred, of course, the underdog gets a sound thrashing. But every once in a while, the minnows have their day, and if you were watching and supporting them then (think Wimbledon versus Liverpool in the 1988 FA Cup Final), you will never forget it.

Waking up thinking it's Friday but realising it is actually Saturday

Is there really any better feeling? OK, so the euphoria only lasts for fleeting seconds before you go back to sleep, but you can't be greedy.

Jay Ward

Ward is not that well known on this side of the Atlantic, but some of his work will ring a bell with people of a certain age. In America he enjoyed success as the producer of many animated series of which the most successful was *Rocky and Bullwinkle*. The adventures of Bullwinkle J. Moose and Rocky the Flying Squirrel are remembered fondly by anyone who grew up in the UK during the '70s when they were widely broadcast, but they actually date from the '50s and '60s. The shows worked on two levels with a sophisticated satirical sub-plot for the parents and very silly storylines and corny jokes for the kids. Or possibly vice versa.

Ward himself was somewhat of an eccentric and loved to make the most of life. For his daughter's wedding, he recreated a summer picnic inside the function room by shipping in real turf complete with ants for added authenticity. He bought a small island near his hometown and named it Moosylvania in honour of Bullwinkle and then went on a campaign to get it recognised as a separate state. This campaign took him all the way to the White House in an attempt to confront President Kennedy, but he ended up being marched off the premises at gunpoint.

Watching English films in foreign countries

It is one of the rare occasions while abroad that you actually know what is going on. Unless it is a David Lynch film you are watching.

Watching television sideways

This almost always means you have managed to convince your parents that you are sick and they have plonked you on the sofa with a glass of Lucozade and some dry toast. A whole day of television awaits you, all of it viewed while lying down. Some of the best days of my childhood were spent in this way.

What a Wonderful World

If any one work represents the sentiment behind this book, then this song is it. Written for Louis Armstrong by Bob Thiele and George David Weiss, it was a flop in the US when it was released in 1967, right in the middle of heightened political and racial tension (clearly listeners didn't get the point). However, it was a #1 hit in the UK. It has since been covered more than thirty times but none come close to the magic, integrity and power of the original. Life really isn't all that bad and this song is all the convincing we need.

Wildlife documentaries

More or less any wildlife documentary does the job. When there is nothing else on the telly there is bound to be one of these on somewhere. And if you manage to pick a good one you can immerse yourself for the next hour. It is rare for television to genuinely entertain and educate at the same time but these shows really do, and the finest of them are never forgotten. Think gorillas, think meerkats, think killer whales.

Window boxes

There is something resoundingly hopeful and uplifting about window boxes. Even without an inch of garden available we don't give up our quest for colour.

Wireless Internet access

No more wires. We can now surf the Internet and send emails from any room in the house, from the train, from the middle of a park, in pubs, in libraries, sitting in the car, sitting on the loo, lying in bed, almost anywhere in fact. The world in your lap.

WOMAD Festival

WOMAD stands for World Of Music, Arts and Dance and has a very simple remit – to bring together and celebrate music, arts and dance from countries and cultures all over the world. This mission manifests itself in many performances, recordings and educational projects but most famously at the many WOMAD festivals around the globe each year.

The UK WOMAD festival has been running since 1982 and is a colourful blend of live music and dance, along with lots and lots of food. The site becomes a temporary village with wigwams and communal tents radiating out from the many stages. It is unashamedly a family event and children are actively made welcome. All racial and cultural barriers are lowered and the entire planet appears to descend upon the fields of southern England.

Working from home

By this, I mean actually working from home, as opposed to 'working from home' with fingers miming quotation marks in the air. The latter is shorthand for sitting on your arse and watching daytime TV or the Test Match and scores highly as an experience in itself. But the former, if approached properly, is a revelation. No commute, no office colleagues asking to borrow your stapler, no meetings to attend. And here is the revelatory part – you get loads more work done.

ALEX JOHNSON IS THE AUTHOR
OF THE WORLD'S ONLY DAILY
BLOG DETAILING THE ADVANTAGES
OF WORKING FROM HOME.

When did you start working from home?

I started in 1994 as a freelance journalist, working out of the spare bedroom of our flat in Battersea. Then we moved to Madrid in 1998 where I worked in a 'traditional' office until 2001 when we came back to England. I started working from home again in the same flat although the spare bedroom had now become my eldest son's bedroom. We moved to St Albans the same year where I worked instead from son number two's bedroom. A year later I bought my shed. That's probably rather more detail than you were really after. Sorry.

What are the advantages as you see them?

Generally, a sense of freedom that you simply don't get in a normal office. I'd much rather be a box fresh, free range homeworker roaming free (or at least in a garden office) than cooped up in a pen, nose to nose with the same battery chicks all day. More specifically:

- A greater control over my time. I still have to work, but I can choose an extremely flexible routine that involves, for example, listening to cricket and playing with my sons, which wouldn't otherwise be possible.
- I can listen to music (which is great since I've never worked with anybody who's shared my interest in early music)
- I choose how my office looks, can wear what I want to work and have a 30-second commute (less if I decide to work on the kitchen table rather than go to the shed).

Tell us a little about Shedworking the blog, and The Shed magazine, if you would be so kind.

The Shed is a free bimonthly pdf magazine for shedworkers and people who work in shedlike atmospheres, a lifestyle (sometimes quite aspirational) title rather than one which features nuts and bolts homeworking subjects such as filling in your tax return. I started it because there is a growing community of shedworkers (and homeworkers in general) whose daily experiences and interests are not catered for by any other publication, indeed who by definition tend to work in relative isolation and are not aware of others in a similar position. I suppose I also started it simply because it is now possible, thanks to broadband uptake and easy pdf production, to put together a decent magazine and distribute it with effectively no overheads. Also, because although I've edited magazines before, I've never been in a position to choose absolutely everything that goes into a magazine. The Shed is mine, all mine, my precious.

The Shedworking and Homeworking blog is a natural extension of the 'brand', again made possible by new technology and its marvellously free nature. The idea of the blog is to provide a daily update of news and items of interest for homeworkers in general, but with a decidedly sheddish slant (e.g. the list of all the UK shed suppliers, which is not available at any other central point). Unbelievably, nobody else does this on a daily basis for homeworkers anywhere in the world.

I could go on about them both for ages, but don't want to bore your socks off.

Shed envy – what's the best homeworking set-up you've seen?

Ooh, that's a very hard one. It might be a bit of a cheat of an answer, but I think you've got to go a long way to beat George Bernard Shaw's revolving hut at Shaw's Corner, just up the road at Ayot St Lawrence, which he could winch round to change the view or improve the light or maybe for a bit of exercise. It had a telephone connection to the house and electrics, and is still in good nick. One of the most admirable is that of Adam Constantine, a designer, who essentially runs a successful carbon-neutral company from his shed in Shrewsbury but in a modestly understated way.

Any famous shedworkers you would care to impress us with?

A small selection might include Andrew Marr, Alison Pearson, Louis de Bernières, Mark Twain, Charles Dickens (though his was more Swiss chalet than shed), Jeanette Winterson, Philip Pullman, Dylan Thomas, William S. Harley and Arthur Davidson, Roald Dahl, Arthur Miller. Er, Linda Barker.

How do you think working from home changes a person?

It deinstitutionalises them. It can also make them fatter if they can't keep away from the fridge (another advantage in working from a shed rather than a kitchen table).

(Alex's Shedworking and Homeworking blog is at http:// shedworking.blogspot.com and you can subscribe to The Shed magazine from there.)

X

Xylophone playing of Sir Patrick Moore

The Sky at Night, BBC television's astronomy programme, was first broadcast in 1957 and has appeared once a month ever since. This makes it the longest running television show on the planet with the same presenter, as every single episode (bar one) has been hosted by Sir Patrick Moore.

Moore's persona is a large part of the appeal of the programme. A man of increasing bulk (he appears to have his own gravitational field), he fills the screen with his cantankerous, eccentric and be-monocled frame. His is a hefty and domineering presence.

But put two lollipop-shaped sticks in his hand (the proper name is 'mallets') and he is transformed into a twinkle-toed musical maestro. Fleet of foot and dainty of finger, he can coax *The Flight of the Bumblebee* out of a row of wooden blocks and bring a smile to the face of even the most curmudgeonly of onlookers.

FASCINATING FACT

Imagine this for a double act: Sir Patrick Moore once performed Saint-Saëns's *The Swan* with Albert Einstein on violin.

Muhumad Yunus

I must confess that I was struggling to find a worthy entry for the letter Y, and then the Nobel Foundation did my job for me. They handed the Nobel Peace Prize to Muhumad Yunus and the Grameen Bank he founded.

Yunus's mission is to eradicate poverty from the planet. He firmly believes that every human being has the potential and right to lead a decent life, not matter what their background or personal means. Based in Bangladesh, his Grameen Bank loans money to the sort of people that no other bank would touch – poor farmers and those in rural communities with no collateral whatsoever. As of 2007, they had seven million borrowers, 97 per cent of whom were women. They lend small amounts of money at very affordable rates to help people buy the tools to farm their land, pay rents or start their own businesses. Despite the severe financial hardships of their borrowers, and the absence of any collateral, Grameen Bank has a much lower default rate than any traditional bank in the western world. It is a system based on trust and a desire to help out our fellow woman and man, and it works.

Zebedee and his sons

In ancient times, during the Roman occupation of the Holy Land, a perfectly pleasant Jewish chap in the Galilee area was quietly going about his business when two of his sons simply upped and left to go fishing with a happy carpenter's son.

Little did he know that nineteen hundred and seventy-four years later no child in the UK could read his name in bible class without some wag shouting 'Boing!' and reducing thirty children to tears of laughter.

Happy days.

Recommended reading

If any of these entries have sparked your curiosity regarding their subjects, then here are some books that may be of interest.

David Attenborough, *Life on Air* (BBC Books). *His excellent autobiography, highly recommended.*

Liam Bailey, *Forever England* (Dewi Lewis). *Collection of photographs taken in and around Bekonscot Model Village. Some look like Edward Hopper paintings.*

Joseph McBride, *Frank Capra* (Faber). *An extensive and fascinating biography.*

Gavin Pretor-Pinney, *The Cloudspotter's Guide* (Sceptre). *No self-respecting cloudspotter can be without this indispensable guide.*

Peter Falk, *Just One More Thing* (Hutchinson). *The man behind the dirty mac tells all.*

W.P. Kinsella, *Shoeless Joe* (Ballantine). *The book that inspired* Field of Dreams. *Only available in the US but quite easy to get hold of from Internet book retailers.*

William J. Higginson, *The Haiku Handbook* (Kodansha Europe). *A great introduction to the art, writing and appreciation of haiku.*

Chuck Jones, *Chuck Amuck* (Farrar Straus Giroux). *A colourful autobiography.*

Werner Holzwarth, *The Story of the Little Mole who knew it was None of His Business* (Chrysalis). *An important moral tale for the kids of today.*

Cheng'en Wu, *Monkey* (Penguin Classics). *The original legend that inspired the TV show.*

Nicey & Wifey, *Nice Cup of Tea and a Sit Down* (Time Warner). *A celebration of tea, biscuit and cake in printed form.*

John Peel and Sheila Ravenscroft, *Margrave of the Marshes* (Corgi). *Autobiography completed after Peel's death by his wife.*

Georges Perec, *Life, a User's Manual* (Vintage). *The most accessible novel from this French genius.*

Oliver Postgate, *Seeing Things* (Pan). *The story of his life and career in television.*

Websites to visit

Many of the entries in the book have official websites that are worth checking out. Here is a list.

The Barnes Foundation – www.barnesfoundation.org
Bekonscot Model Village – www.bekonscot.com
Cloud Appreciation Society – www.cloudappreciationsociety.org
Omlet (the people who make eglus) – www.omlet.co.uk
The Fat Duck – www.fatduck.co.uk
Flaming Lips – www.flaminglips.com
Free Hugs – www.freehugscampaign.org
Guildo Horn – www.guildo-horn.com
Ice Hotel – www.icehotel.com
Innocent – www.innocentdrinks.co.uk
J-List – www.jlist.com
The Landmark Trust – www.landmarktrust.org.uk
LibraryThing – www.librarything.com
Nice Cup of Tea and a Sit Down – www.nicecupofteaandasitdown.com
Peter Payne's Blog – www.peterpayne.net
The Pudding Club – www.puddingclub.com
A Quarter Of – www.aquarterof.co.uk

Shedworking – http://shedworking.blogspot.com
Smallfilms – www.smallfilms.co.uk
WOMAD – www.womad.org

Acknowledgements

Just a quick thank you to the lovely people at The Friday Project for getting behind my book and sharing my belief that the world is not quite as shite as some people would have you believe. Clare, Heather, Clare, Maddy and Scott are as fine a bunch of people as I could have hoped to work with (Clare Weber deserves special mention as editor of the book you now hold in your hand).

A big round of applause to the individuals who agreed to be interviewed by me for the book. Your input is greatly appreciated and I owe you one.

Finally, thanks and love to my family for giving me the time to write this book.

Steve Stack
stevestack@hotmail.co.uk